NEVER GIVE UP

E.Z. JONES

For more info contact:

E.Z. Jones
P.O. Box 2400
Sugar Land, TX 77487

ez@ezjones.com

DEDICATION

I dedicate this book to my wife, Lena. Thank you, honey, for the countless hours you spent making this book a reality because without you, it would not exist. There are no words to express how much I love you. The first forty-four years of my life before I met you were filled with accomplishment. But the last forty-four years we have experienced together have been filled with adventure.

And the best is yet to come!

ACKNOWLEDGEMENTS

I want to acknowledge my precious mother, Ida Lorena Epps, who has been in heaven for many years. I want to acknowledge my daughter in the Lord, Debra Hayes, who left this earth much sooner than I desired. These two women, born decades apart, were both so full of love and generosity.

I also want to acknowledge Lena's mother, Mary Teresa Pizzitola and Lena's spiritual mother, Mickie Winborn. These amazing women made lasting deposits in our lives for which I am forever grateful.

To my two sons, Clif and Paul Michael, I am so proud of you both. May you leave nothing undone of all God intends in your lives.

To my spiritual sons and daughters over the years who are still being added to today, may you be forces for God in the world and make a difference everywhere you go.

To all those who have supported our ministry, you are partners in every milestone and every miracle. To our church congregation both past and present, I am so grateful for all the amazing things God has done and is doing in our midst!

WITH SPECIAL THANKS

And last but not least, I would like to give special thanks to my friend Perry Hardwick for his generous support in publishing this book.

TABLE OF CONTENTS

FOREWORDS

Reading through the pages of this book, I was riveted by each story! There were moments where I found myself getting choked up, while other moments chuckling and smiling.

I've had the privilege of knowing E.Z. and Lena Jones since late 1981. When E.Z shares the story of our first meeting in this book, it brought back so many deep and fond memories. In fact, they have had a significant impact during many of the critical junctures in my early walk in the Lord, as well as in the trajectory of my life in ministry.

I've often said that, "Relationships define and influence our destinies".

E.Z. and Lena have had an indelible impact and have been part of providential landmarks in my life along the way. Some of what I'm involved in around the globe today has connection to their love and belief in me over the years. They have been spiritual parents to many lives, including mine. Words cannot adequately express the value or importance of their investment. I am forever grateful!

Read through this book, fully assured that you too, have a storyline of greater purpose and destiny that God is formulating through your own life. May you find yourself recognizing the redemptive purposes and the great and abounding grace of God for you, provoking you into the faith walk He intends for you.

Doug Stringer, founder/president
Turning Point Ministries International
Somebody Cares America / International, Houston, Texas

E.Z. Jones has been a close friend and a brother in Christ for more than thirty years. He has ALWAYS been there for me during the many different seasons of my life. He encouraged me when I was discouraged and gave me solid godly advice when I was not sure what to do. He has consistently prayed for and checked on how my family and I are doing for almost four decades. E.Z. always directed me to the Word of God and assured me he knew that was the only real truth. I love E.Z. and Lena Jones and have been so highly blessed by them and their amazing ministry. But you know what? I have witnessed E.Z. doing this same thing for so many others and for anyone who needed any kind of help. I praise God for E.Z. Jones, a man who has a pure heart of love for God and for his neighbor.

Tim Hallmark
Hallmark Sports Training
Sports Performance Trainer for Evander Holyfield and other world-class athletes

I have always admired E.Z. and Lena Jones for how they love God and serve Him. I think E.Z.'s book will be a great blessing to you.

Dodie Osteen
Founder, Lakewood Church

The first professional hockey team I ever played on was the Houston Aeros of the WHA and it was owned by E.Z. Jones. How ironic that 20 years later, when I came back to coach the new Houston Aeros of the IHL, E.Z. became my pastor, friend and father figure. Whenever I had to make major decisions, it was E.Z. who I called for advice. When I was coaching in Laredo, Texas and the game was close, I would call him to pray for my team. I cannot count the number of times I owed my wins to God and E.Z. Jones. Besides my immediate family, E.Z. is the one man to whom I always say "I love you" before I hang up the phone or walk away from him.

So.... E.Z., I love you!

Terry Ruskowski
World Hockey Association Hall of Fame
Former Professional Hockey Player
Former Professional Hockey Coach/General Manager

HEADLINES AND HIGHROLLERS

Opening the Houston Chronicle on the morning of May 3, 1975 I immediately saw my name in one of the headlines. Before computers and the internet, most people had daily home delivery of the newspaper and read it every morning just like I was doing. It was my forty-second birthday, and reading that headline made me stop and reflect.

Fifteen years earlier, after graduating from Trinity University, I went to work for Gold Bond Building Materials. They sold things like paneling, sheetrock, insulation and everything else it took to build homes, apartments and office buildings. I had a company car and an expense account, and made three hundred sixty-five dollars a month, which was great pay at the time. My days began early in the morning at 7:00 a.m. breakfast staff meetings. Everyone was given six-month sales quotas with exactly how much they expected us to produce in sales. Some of us exceeded our quotas, but then the executives took the business we worked so hard to get and gave it to others who weren't even trying to make their numbers. That seemed wrong to me, and I didn't like it, but it was just how they did things.

While working at Gold Bond, one of my best clients was Norman Norwood. Norman was the owner of Monarch Homes, one of the largest homebuilders in Houston, Texas. Since my degree was in pre-law and home-building, I was familiar with everything it took to build houses. Norman had great crews who specialized in various aspects of the trade, but he lacked men who had an overall education in homebuilding. Several guys I had gone to school with had their home-building degrees but they were still in need of a job, so I connected them with Norman. When a few of them were hired on at Monarch as superintendents, they sent business my way. Needless to say, I routinely met my six-month quota in ninety days.

With new construction springing up all over Houston, I was curious how guys who knew relatively little about construction were able to obtain all their financing. I began asking questions to see what I could find out and I learned that a good mortgage broker was the key. After meeting one of the mortgage brokers, it was obvious to me that he needed more insight into the construction process to understand how to approve his loan draws. I teamed up with him, knowing I could easily locate builders in need of loans. Then I'd connect them with this broker, who provided funding for their projects. As draw requests came in, I would help the broker assess the completion percentages and it was a beneficial situation for everybody. After a while, I discussed doing a project of my own with that broker. He told me to find a location for my first project, and he would provide the funds.

I didn't realize it then, but a whole new phase of my life was about to begin. From 1963 to 1972, I ended up building eleven apartment complexes, ranging from 32 units to 400 units, all across South Texas.

It started in 1963 when I noticed in the newspaper that the National Aeronautics and Space Administration (NASA) would soon be built in Webster, Texas, south of Houston. It immediately occurred to me that there would be an influx of employees who would need housing. I knew about a prime parcel of land there that hadn't yet been listed for sale because few people were aware of NASA's plans. So, I immediately went to the property owner and bought the land. That's where I built my first apartments, a small 32-unit project. It wasn't hard for me to figure out where housing was going to be needed. All my life I had learned to think ahead just to survive, and maybe now it was going to pay off.

I then started looking for other areas where people would need apartment projects. After reading that World War II babies, now at college age, were enrolling in universities with limited dormitory space, I had my idea. There was a shortage of dormitory space at Texas A&M in College Station, Texas, so I drove up to A&M and met with the president of the university. "Sir, if I build apartments near the school, can your students live in them?" I asked. He said, "Yes, our junior and senior students and graduate students can, as long as they are nicely built and well-maintained."

I found out there was a piece of property for sale next door to the mayor of Bryan, Texas. I was happy to locate some land, but then the realtor, an elderly gentleman, told me that it had a big old house on it. "Wait a minute!" I said. "I don't need a parcel of land with a big old house on it. I would have the expense of tearing it down." He said, "It's where the first president of Texas A&M University once lived. It's filled with antiques. If you offer the antique dealers in the area those antiques, I know they'll tear down the building for you. They will gladly help you. It's a win/win."

It made sense to me. I found the antique dealers anxious to accept my offer. Before I knew it, they emptied the house of the costly antiques, but they left the house standing there!

It was a first for me since I knew nothing about demolishing a large building. However, I eventually tore it down and never bought another piece of property with a building on it.

Once the apartment complex there was completed, I began to look at other universities.

I went to Huntsville, Texas, the home of Sam Houston State University. Their president had once been at Alvin Junior College, and I was familiar with him. I asked him if I could build apartments for his students. He wrote me a letter stating what the A&M president had said, that the university needed the additional housing and their students could stay in them. It was easy for me to get loans once lenders read their letters.

One day I received a letter from a lady who was head of Continental Airlines stewardesses. She was concerned because many of their stewardesses, now referred to as flight attendants, were still living near Hobby Airport. It was on the south side of Houston, requiring them to drive 45 minutes to the new Intercontinental Airport on the north side of town. I asked her if she would state in writing that the stewardesses would live in my apartments if I built them. She said she definitely would. So, I sent the letter she wrote to a small insurance company in Mobile, Alabama, and got a loan to cover the project. Once again, I was building apartments in Houston.

I ended up building apartments for several universities around the state of Texas as well as projects all across Houston. The biggest project I owned was about 400 units. One of the locations in Houston had an on-premise "nightclub" for residents, complete with dance floors, music, and disco mirror balls. It was the first of its kind. Such clubs proved to be quite a drawing card for tenants during the sixties and early seventies. Being innovative was something I enjoyed, and I felt like I added some allure to apartment living.

I visited my projects regularly to see how they were being maintained. But when I visited, I dressed in some old zip-up one-piece coveralls. Most of the employees thought I was a maintenance man sent over from another project checking on things. They paid little attention to me. Being "in disguise" allowed me to see what the workers were doing without anyone suspecting I was the owner. When projects were still under construction, it was quite enlightening to see which contractors were actually getting the job done. Even though I went unnoticed for many months, at the end of the year, we had our big company-wide Christmas party. Some folks were shocked when they realized who I really was, and my incognito days were over.

After building some commercial office buildings, word began to spread, and my name became well-known in the city. The September 1972 issue of the Houston Business Journal featured my picture front and center on their cover with an article entitled "The Saga of E.Z. Jones." It went into great detail about how I had built hundreds of apartments all over Houston and in nearby cities. There were several anecdotes from my life and all kinds of colorful stories! They wrote about how I had forty women working for me to run all my properties; the writer said I was a "female chauvinist" when I told him I got a lot more done with women employees.

Shortly after that article was written, I received a call from a friend named Bill Lund, who wanted to meet with me. Bill was from Minnesota, and he loved to ice skate. He said to me, "E.Z., I think we need an ice-skating rink in Houston." Since I knew Joe McDermott, who built Town and Country Shopping Center, I decided to pay him a visit. He knew a whole lot about commercial real estate in Houston. After exchanging pleasantries, I said, "Joe, I'm looking for a location to build an ice-skating rink. Do you know of any place?"

"E.Z.," he said, "I'll tell you where to build your ice rink if you tell me where you got that shirt."

I was wearing an expensive monogrammed shirt made for me by Hamilton Shirt Shop. Once I told him where he could buy a shirt like mine, he let me know about a place they had been using for a farmers' market. They were not going to use it anymore and he encouraged me to take a look at it.

Taking an architect with us, Bill and I went to see it. We had to raise the ceilings and upgrade several things, but instead of building one rink, we ended up building *two*. First, we laid out a small rink and then a larger one beside it as if you were looking down on a frozen lake. Then we built cafés around the rinks like the chalets you might see in Switzerland; it was basically a food court concept but well before its time.

My friend Bill Lund started managing the rinks for me, and one day he told me we needed a Zamboni.

I said, "A what?"

Bill informed me it was one of those large machines you drive around the rink to shave the ice to keep it smooth and safe for skating. But I was shocked when he told me how much it was going to cost.

One day I dropped in and saw some elderly people sweeping the ice with brooms. "Hey, wait a minute! I thought we spent all that money on a Zamboni machine to clean the ice. Now you have these old guys out here sweeping it with brooms!" I said to Bill.

Bill often called me "Country" as a nickname. He said, "Country, that's called curling." The sport of curling is relatively unknown in most of the U.S. It's a little like shuffleboard on ice. Each player slides stones on the ice toward a target area while a partner stays ahead of the stone, sweeping the ice with a broom to remove anything that would hinder it. It was an unknown concept to somebody like me from the cotton patches of Oklahoma.

Soon after I built the ice rinks, the Houston Aeros Hockey Team franchise came to town. The owner was an architect named Paul

Deneau. He asked if his team could practice at our place. I said, "Yes, you can if you'll allow me to use the Aeros to advertise my new rink." Surprisingly, he agreed! Since he was an architect and I was a builder, we got along quite well.

One day in 1973, Paul asked if I'd like to buy some stock in his hockey team and help him promote the Houston Aeros. I said, "Yes!" It sounded like a perfect fit to me. I began to buy stock in the Aeros, and before long, I became the Vice President and was part-owner of the company. He retained his position as President/CEO and part-owner. We would travel together to the owner's meetings all over the United States and Canada--to every city where there was a hockey team.

As an owner of the team, one thing I enjoyed was watching the hockey players practice. They were incredible on the ice, so fast and so strong. Gordie Howe was the most well-known hockey player in the world, and the fact that his two sons were playing alongside him on the team was an anomaly. Because of this father-son trio, we became known far and wide. Gordie and I became really close friends. While the Howes could be rough and rowdy on the ice, they were actually quite gentlemanly once the skates and jerseys were off. After the games, we'd enjoy going downtown to the old White Hall Hotel for prime rib. The cooks and waitstaff would save the best cuts for us and look forward to our coming by.

The people who had started the World Hockey League decided next to launch World Team Tennis. Since I was doing so well with hockey, I quickly wrote a $50,000 check and purchased World Team Tennis's first franchise. My team was going to be called the Hurricanes. But while we were in Palm Springs having a meeting about the team, a newspaper reporter in Houston referred to my team as "The E-Z Riders." By the time we got back, there was so much coverage with that name, we went with it and became known as the E-Z Riders. I grew up being called Zade, which was my middle name, but it was customary to go by your first two initials in the military. Since age 17, when I was in the Marines, I have gone by my initials, E.Z.

When I attended Trinity University in the late '50s in San Antonio, I had become friends with Trinity's tennis coach, Clarence Mabry. He had a phenomenal student tennis player from Australia who had become the number one ranked tennis player in the world. I contacted Coach Clarence to ask if we could get this player, John Newcombe, for our tennis team. I thought it would be difficult because he had signed with the ATP (Association of Tennis Professionals), a unionized company. But to my surprise, John signed a five-year contract with us, and I signed a personal guarantee for his salary. With the number one tennis player in the world on our team, everyone else wanted to play for us. Soon we had an incredible roster of star players. And World Team Tennis ended up with 16 teams throughout the United States and in Hawaii. When the famous Billie Jean King vs. Bobby Riggs tennis match was held in Houston in September of 1973, my team was instrumental in arranging and handling the logistics.

My life became a whirlwind of games and players and practices and then newspaper interviews about those same things. Growing up, I had always loved sports. Now my life was filled with two sports, but as an owner instead of as a player. It was quite exciting being in the middle of it all! We had E-Z Rider pins and banners and posters, and my name was on everything. One entire closet at my home looked like a sports memorabilia shop. There were hockey pucks that won the winning point in championship games and hockey sticks signed by the most famous players in the sport, three of whom played on my team. I had Houston Aeros and E-Z Riders caps, shirts, and windbreakers, and I became pretty impressed with myself.

I traveled from place to place in private planes and helicopters while attending all the sporting events and meeting with people I'd never met before. I was now living in the lap of luxury. Not many of these upper-class society folks had come from a background of poverty like I had. I was, as we say in the South, "in high cotton!" I got involved with lots of projects in our city and became the topic of many magazine and newspaper articles. Being interviewed on radio and television became commonplace because I now owned two professional sports teams, apartment projects, and commercial properties. Whether it was in the sports section or the business section, I was generally being written about for one reason or another.

Then the Houston Aeros became the very first sports team to win a world championship in Houston. And to top it off, we won not just one but two world championships, back-to-back in 1974 and 1975. We got press coverage all across the nation! After our first world hockey championship, I received my prized possession, a diamond-encrusted championship ring engraved with my initials. Then they gave me a President's Rolex watch after winning the second one, and life didn't seem like it could get any better. The championships were quite exciting for the entire city. Since World Team Tennis attracted lots of movie stars and society types, I started running with some of the world's wealthiest people. The maître d's at the fanciest restaurants all knew me by name.

Lamar Hunt was legendary in the eyes of many people, and we became great friends. He was a son of H.L. Hunt, one of the world's richest men, and was quite an amazing man himself. At age 26, Lamar wanted to purchase a National Football League (NFL) expansion team, but he got turned down. Then he tried to buy an existing team to move them to Dallas and also got turned down. Undaunted, Lamar got some investors together to launch the American Football League (AFL) as competition. After trying to establish a Dallas team, called the Texans, he decided to take the team he founded to Kansas City. There, they became the Kansas City Chiefs, a successful football franchise to this day. But I got to know him because of his ownership of the American Tennis Professional (ATP) league. His general manager visited me regularly, and Lamar and I developed a great relationship.

Not only was I hobnobbing with business elites, but with politicians also. I became personal friends with the governor of the State of Texas. We produced many celebrity tournaments, and dozens of these well-to-do people attended. I had never known much about wealthy people or what they did. But I was a fast learner, and it sure didn't take me long to acclimate! Since I was well-known in both real estate circles and sports circles, I was catered to everywhere I went. I became accustomed to hearing, "Mr. Jones, what can I do for you?" At the fanciest restaurants, waiters would say, "Mr. Jones, what would you like the chef to make for you today? Anything you like!" I started talking seriously about running for governor of Texas, one of my lifelong goals, and I'm not sure if I was just very confident or extremely prideful.

But I'll give you some great advice--don't kick the ladder out from under yourself that you used to climb up on--because you never know when you might need it to get back down!

Because I was A LONG way from where I had started. A very, very long way.

Flour Sacks and Pickin' Cotton

I was born on May 3, 1933, in Cotton County, Oklahoma. With five brothers and two sisters, we all lived in a two-room sharecropper's house in the country. Family planning didn't seem to exist back then. Most families were large like ours, and people raised their children to help them work their farms. A brother had died before I was born, and a stepbrother would come later, so I was one of ten kids.

On the farm, everyone, from the oldest to the youngest, had their chores. As soon as I could walk, I helped feed the chickens. By the time I was in the first grade, I worked slopping the hogs and milking the cows. By the second grade, I had learned how to drive a mule around a hay baler and did it from sunrise until sunset during hay season. Nowadays, that would be considered child abuse, but it was just part of a regular workday back then.

Making butter was one of my jobs. After I milked the cows, I'd skim the thick cream off the top of the milk, place it in a half-gallon fruit jar and "churn it" into butter. Mother would make biscuits and serve them with cream gravy. I was only six years old, but I understood what it took for our family to eat, hard work and lots of it. We butchered our own hogs to have bacon and raised our own chickens so there would be eggs. We raised cows to have milk and butter.

Our farm-fresh breakfasts were delicious, and I loved to wake up to the smell of Mother's homemade cinnamon rolls. She'd roll out the dough and bake the rolls in our wood-burning oven. Then she'd place them on a flat screened-in window-ledge that extended out into the open air to cool. To me, they were a sight to see!

She also placed the pies and cakes she cooked on that same ledge. When I couldn't resist, even though I knew I risked getting spanked, I'd stick my finger under that screen and get a little "taste" of her latest baked item. When my deed got discovered, I would get a spanking with my dad's old razor strap she had kept for that purpose. She would then explain why she had spanked me, tell me she loved me, and hug me afterward. But at least I got a taste before everybody else did.

While it was lots of hard work, childhood on the farm was not short on adventures and new experiences. We walked most places, including to school and back each day.

Walters, Oklahoma, the county seat and the closest town to our farm, was 22 miles away. Since we didn't own a car, we had no way to travel that far. It was several years before I was allowed to go to town. I remember the day my brother and I rode a wagon to town atop a bale of cotton. I had twenty-five cents in my pocket, and I thought I would buy out Walters, Oklahoma with it. The truth is, I immediately spent almost all of my quarter on a sack full of candy. I thought it was the greatest thing that had ever happened to me. I ate way too much, of course. But I did manage to bring some home so that everybody could share in my treasure.

On Sundays, Mother would clean us up, get us dressed, and take us to the church in the old wagon. On certain Sundays, they'd have all-day singing and dinner on the ground. But it was a little more like all-day eating and singing on the ground. Every lady in the church would bring her specialty, and we'd eat until we could hold no more. Of course, the pies, puddings, and cakes were unforgettable. I always enjoyed going to church, and I loved the singing at the evening services.

Our Christmases in those days were very simple. With a family as large as ours and with so little income, expectations were small.

For example, an extravagant Christmas present might consist of a matchbox car. Now mind you, I mean a real matchbox that holds large kitchen matches. We'd push a wooden pencil through each end of an empty matchbox to make the axles. Then we'd stick one of Mother's empty sewing spools on the end of each pencil for the wheels. I played in the dirt for hours on end with my treasured cars.

I remember two times at Christmas when the county, trying to help poor families, gifted me with one apple and one orange. Since we didn't grow those on the farm, they were a special treat for me, and I was excited to have them.

Like every other country home in those days, we had an outhouse as there was no inside plumbing. We had "running water," but not as you might think. We would have to "run" and get water every day when we came home from school. As kids, we'd carry the buckets to the well, pump them full with the hand pump, then lug them back to the house. It was an everyday occurrence, so we never considered it an inconvenience. But then, the word convenience was not even in our vocabulary.

Every few days, we'd fill a wash pot with water. After building a log fire underneath to get it hot, Mother would fill the washtub with warm water, and we children would take turns bathing. Yep, all of us in the same water! The younger kids, like me, were last. Keep in mind, we didn't know any better, and it would have been much too hard to do water changes anyway.

When Dad butchered a hog, Mother would render the fat and make our soap. We used Mother's homemade lye soap to take a bath, shampoo our hair, wash our dishes, and launder our clothes. Then we would hang the laundry on the clothesline behind the house to dry. Unlike today, we had to watch the weather closely. If we noticed rain approaching, we'd quickly run outside and grab the laundry. But honestly, the clothes smelled and felt cleaner after having dried in the sun than they do today with our electric and gas dryers.

Of course, we had no electricity at all. We used coal-oil lamps to light the house at night.

Mother was an excellent cook, and she did all her cooking on the wood-burning stove in the kitchen. We grew our vegetables in our large family garden, and our job as kids was to weed and hoe. Then at harvest time, Mother would fire up her kitchen stove and can the vegetables in jars. I hated cleaning those Ball fruit jars, so the canning season was my least favorite time of year. Mother would cook the fruit and vegetables we'd grown, then spoon them into her canning jars. The canning jars were heated in hot water until a vacuum formed. Once the jars cooled down, we would tote them to the storm cellar in our backyard.

Sadly, I only have one memory of my dad, when walking about a mile and back with him to get our mail. Dad's eyesight was poor because he had been mustard-gassed fifteen years earlier while serving in Germany during World War I. When I was four years old, my dad and his friend, Shorty Feets, went into town for supplies. Mother said that Dad and Shorty stopped at a store located next to a hill. Dad went in to buy some things that he planned to bring home.

In the days before people used moving vans, a man moving his family's belongings had hitched a cotton trailer behind his car. As he drove down the hill, the trailer broke loose and rapidly careened down the incline as it gained speed, then flipped over. At that moment, without warning, coming out of the store, it hit my dad. Shorty came out of the store and didn't see him anywhere. After searching all over, he found him helplessly pinned directly underneath the cotton trailer.

They carefully extracted my dad from beneath the trailer and took him to the hospital in Lawton, Oklahoma. But the hospital wouldn't treat him until my mother could get there to explain if and how she would pay for their services. My mom was 20 miles away and without transportation, so by the time she arrived and rushed in, he died in her arms.

After the burial, a man from the county told Mother, "Mrs. Jones, you need to put these kids up for adoption. You have too many of them to care for." The country was still in the Great Depression, and he didn't think she would be able to support such a large family alone. My feisty mother replied, "Sir, when I die, someone can adopt them, but not a moment before!" My mom told us how Jesus appeared to her one night at the end of her ironing board and let her know everything was going to be okay. She invited my grandmother to move in with us, and our grandmother would watch us kids while Mother did most of the adult farm work required to keep things going.

When Mother went into Walters for groceries, she would hitchhike. She'd walk down the road toward town carrying a big burlap sack. Before long, a kind driver would stop and offer her a ride; then later, Mother would hitchhike home. When she arrived home in the evening, her burlap sack filled with purchases, we would watch her unload it all. Often there would be extra flour she bought just because of the pattern on the cloth flour sacks. Our mom used those empty sacks to make our underwear or shorts. Once, she even made a shirt.

We may have had very little, but we always had our mother's love. At night, she would place a lighted coal-oil lantern on the table and read the Bible to us. The next morning she'd get up before the rest of us and begin her day's work.

Then mother got remarried to a man named Guy, and he became my stepdad when I was about eleven. Guy drove a '29 Chevrolet that he redesigned, so it had a small pickup-style bed in the back. One day, we loaded it with our possessions, and we moved to Goodlett, Texas, which is northwest of Wichita Falls. We moved into a vacant garage with a dirt floor where mechanics used to work on people's cars because we couldn't find anything else we could afford. We still had no indoor plumbing, so we used an outhouse in the back for a toilet. Of course, toilet paper was a thing in the future. Like most folks in those days, we would tear pages out of our thick Sears and Roebuck catalog for that purpose. We couldn't buy anything out of the catalog anyway. My mother used to say, "We are so poor we can't even pay attention… and if steamboat whistles were selling for a penny apiece, we couldn't even buy an echo!"

Once in Goodlett, we began to pick cotton. We would get up early in the morning and go to the field with big cotton sacks. Cotton picking sacks were heavy canvas bags, 6 foot, 7 ½ foot, and 9-foot lengths. They had shoulder straps. We'd put the strap over our shoulder and drag the sacks behind us as we walked down each cotton row. Each bag would hold 40- to 45-pounds of cotton. We walked bent over to pull the cotton from its bolls and drop them in the bag, which was quite painful to our backs. A workday like that would be challenging under any circumstances, but in Texas' hot summer sun, it could be excruciating. Not only was it difficult on our backs, but our fingers would get bloodied from pulling the cotton from their prickly hard-sun-dried bolls. When the sack got heavy and full, which took anywhere from two to four hours depending on the field, we would carry it to the cotton trailer to be weighed and emptied. Then we'd repeat the process over and over 'till it was dark.

We moved around a lot and one place we lived was Ruidoso, New Mexico, where we lived in a fairly decent cabin. My sister,

Faye, would walk with me about half a mile to school each day and to church on Sunday. It wasn't bad, except when it snowed. The best thing was that at last, I had shoes. I had received my first pair when I was nine years old but until then, being barefooted was all I knew. In Ruidoso, I got a job picking apples because there were lots of apple orchards there. When there weren't apples to pick, I worked stacking green lumber. Two of my older brothers drove logging trucks.

My family later moved to Fulton, Texas, on the Gulf of Mexico, between Victoria and Corpus Christi, Texas. I got a job "heading shrimp," which was a misnomer, it seemed to me. We were removing the heads from the shrimp. We weren't heading them; we were de-heading them. It was an awful, smelly job and I had to wear those same smelly clothes to school! That's when I decided I had to make something of myself, somehow. It embarrassed me when kids would call me names, especially when they called me the dirty snotty-nosed Jones kid! I vowed that one day I'd get as far away from poverty as I could.

After a couple of years, I was old enough to get a job on a shrimp boat that a friend of ours owned. Working as a roustabout (a deckhand), I remember one day when we went out into the bay and caught a huge haul of shrimp. I got so seasick I wanted to die. But hard work didn't scare me, and I was determined to show the boat captain that I could finish what I started, so I stayed at it.

Shortly after that, we moved down the road to Rockport, Texas, where we lived on a ranch about three and a half miles from town. I got an old bicycle that I would ride into town, and after school, I mowed lawns. Then I'd wash dishes at the café and ride my bike the three and a half miles back home. Funny, I had applied for the job of "busboy," thinking I'd be riding a bus all day. I really liked the sound of that. But once hired, I discovered the job was cleaning off tables and washing dishes. Since I needed the money, I still took the job.

When I was in the eighth and ninth grades, I was able to get jobs from people in Victoria who owned summer homes down in Rockport. Mother would tend their flower beds, and I'd mow their lawns after school 'till dark. Then I'd get on my bicycle again and ride the three and a half miles back to Bailey's Ranch where we lived. With the money Mom and I earned, we decided to buy some land. I asked my seventh-grade teacher, Miss Ruth, if she wanted to sell the thirty-five acres she owned. We passed by it every morning and night on the way to do yards and on the way home. Amazingly, she agreed to sell it to us on an installment plan. We would pay it off with our yard earnings, but I also had an idea to start selling dirt off the land at $1 a load. I could even help to load it. Before you know it, my plan took off. Between that and leasing it by the acre after oil was struck in the area, mom and I ended up owning the land free and clear. We divided it into several lots, measuring each lot off ourselves with an old 100-foot metal measuring tape. We then started selling off parcels here and there for a profit. So, I did my first real estate development at age 14, and my first partner was my mother.

That same year, I started working at a service station. When somebody pulled up to a pump, I would come out and wash their windshield and check the air in their tires while I filled their tank with gasoline. I would check the water in the radiator and battery and even check the oil if they asked me.

The following year, I got my commercial driver's license. Back then, if there was a sufficient family need, a young person could get a "hardship license" a year or two early. My life consisted of work, and I had plenty of hardship--well, jobs to help bring in money.

So, I could now drive a dump truck in the summer. I went to Ingleside, Texas, where they were tearing down what had been an Exxon property. Back then, Exxon was known as the Humble Oil Company. I'd load the truck, then drive back toward Rockport, where I'd dump it near the water's edge, then repeat the process over and over. I also learned to drive a bulldozer, and I thought I knew how to do everything, even though I didn't. But I was working harder than many adult men.

I worked really hard almost every day, but I also practiced my sports. Waking up early, I'd ride my bicycle to the school and start practicing. I played tennis, basketball, football, and I boxed. As the middleweight Golden Glove champion at that time, I was in excellent physical condition, and I worked out all the time. Even though I lettered in every sport, my mother still made my shorts and shirts out of flour sacks. When I won the middleweight championship, all the guys saw those shorts I was wearing. They went home afterward and asked their mothers to make them flour sack shorts. I thought that was funny, but they were serious about it. Soon, they were wearing flour-sack shorts, so I became a trend-setter, and Mother became famous.

FOOTBALL FEATS AND FRONTPAGE FAILURE

I played football during both my freshman and sophomore years in high school. At the end of my sophomore year in May, I had my 17th birthday. Two older men with whom I worked had served as Marines in World War II in Guadalcanal and Iwo Jima. One day, they told me, "We're not going to be here this summer. We're going to California." Wow, I thought, I've never been west of Carlsbad, New Mexico. When I asked why they were going to California, they said they were Marine reservists and had to report for two-week duty each summer.

I had just gone over to Corpus Christi, Texas, to see the movie "Sands of Iwo Jima," a 1950 war film starring John Wayne. It was one of the most incredible things I'd ever seen. So, when they said they were in the Marine reserves, I was all ears. I immediately asked how I could join the Corp. They said that I had to be 18 years old. I was bound and determined to be a Marine. So, in May 1950, when I turned 17, having finished my sophomore year in high school, I got permission from my mother to enlist. I lied about my age and joined the United States Marine Corps. I thought I would only be in the reserves, but I found myself on active duty when the Korean war began.

At first, the Corp sent me to the Marine Air Reserve Training Detachment at Naval Air Station (NAS), Memphis, Tennessee. That was disheartening because, having seen John Wayne's movie, I wanted to go to Korea. After finishing my Tennessee assignment, they sent me to school at the Naval Amphibious Base in Little Creek, Virginia. There I spent time in martial arts training and hours on the rifle range. The harder I tried to get to Korea, the further away it seemed they were sending me. Looking back on it, I think it was all a result of my mother's prayers to keep me safe. During the war, mothers were given U.S. flags with added stars for each son they had in the military. My mom had six stars on her flag. I spent two years in the Marines on active duty and went to many places, but never once did I get to Korea.

When I received an honorable discharge from the Marines, at age 19, I returned to South Texas. While I still had three more years in the Marine Reserves, I was free to resume my life. My cousin was a driller on a Phillips 66 Oil Company offshore oil rig, so he hired me to do manual labor, or "roughneck." I worked hard seven days a week and have scars to this day on my forearm where some drill pipe stabbed clean through it. It isn't a job for the weak or the faint of heart. But I noticed that the engineers who visited our rig would examine a few things that we had done, then they'd go back to their fancy quarters and sleep. I began to think, "Man, that's what I want to do. I want a job like that!" So, I decided I would go to college.

I hadn't finished high school, but as a veteran, I was able to enroll at Texas A&I in Kingsville, Texas, an hour south of Corpus Christi. I signed up for trigonometry, algebra, calculus, and other engineering classes. It seemed to me that's what I needed to do to become an engineer. I walked into class the first day and was shocked! The instructor was my Marine Commanding Officer. He said, "You sit right there, and don't you get up!" I'm just grateful I passed his class!

Because I'd been working on the offshore drilling rig, I was in great shape and started playing football immediately. But I didn't like the coach there, so I withdrew before I finished one semester.

While visiting my brother in Victoria, I learned that the legendary Rusty Russell coached their football team. He had coached SMU when they beat Notre Dame in 1951. I'd won a bet while in the Marine Corps when Coach Russell's SMU Mustangs with Doak Walker and Kyle Rote beat the Notre Dame team. Some of my buddies in the service were giving 100 to 1 odds and others 50 to 1 odds that Notre Dame would win and I just decided I'd bet on SMU. When amazingly, SMU won, I was stuffing cash in my pockets. Many of the guys now had no money to send to their wives and families back home, which is what they did every time they got paid. I was single and decided to call a meeting the next day in my tent. Every guy in our company had to bring an envelope addressed to their wife or family and they couldn't figure out what in the world I was doing, but they all showed up. As I gave each one of them every penny of their money back, I sealed it in the envelope and stamped it for mailing. I was given favorable treatment after that even though I was a low-ranking corporal and some of them were sergeants or lieutenants.

Coach Russell was impressive and since I'd bet on him and won, I couldn't wait to be a player on his team. Immediately, I enrolled at Victoria Junior College on a football scholarship. Although I had not been through my junior and senior years in high school, I had enough experience to enroll because I served in the Marine Corps and roughnecked for three years. It had been five years since I'd played football, but I was sure I wanted to play for Coach Russell. I lettered in football both years at Victoria Junior College. Then during my second year, I became team captain and all-college favorite.

One day at practice, while jogging near the stadium, I noticed a subdivision being built. I found out that The Foremen Brothers were the developers, and I watched their progress with interest. Then one day, I saw a guy I recognized from one of my classes attaching asbestos siding. In 1953, brick siding wasn't as popular as asbestos siding.

I stopped and asked him about what I had seen him doing.
He explained that his brothers were builders and he was working for them putting on the asbestos siding. He added that he contracted most of it out. As we talked it became clear that he made good money doing it.
I inquired, "Can anybody get a job doing that?"
He said, "Well, I'd have to train them to do it, but it wouldn't take long."
"Could you train me to do it?" I quickly asked.
He said he would and that I could probably make about $2.50 an hour.
Remember, that was back in the days when 50 cents per hour was good pay.
So, I said, "Okay, I'd like to learn to do that."

He taught me how to install the siding, and I worked very hard. Toward the end of the year, he was about to graduate from our two-year junior college. One day, he asked if I would like to take his position and work for his brother doing the contracting. He mentioned that I would need to find a couple of guys and teach them how to do it. I told him I could do that.
He said, "If you find some guys and you pay them $2.50 an hour, they will be thrilled."
I said, "Okay. Sure."

When he left, he gave me his position. I went over to the part of Victoria where most of the Hispanic people lived. I saw a group of guys, stopped, and said, "Look, do any of you guys want a job making $2.50 an hour?" I continued, "It's a good, clean job." One said, "Well, what do you want me to do, kill somebody?"
"No," I laughed, "I just want to teach you how to put asbestos siding on houses."

They said, "Okay, we see that done all the time."
I explained, "Well, I'll tell you what. I'll give two of you a job and train you how to do it."
They agreed.

The Foreman Brothers were paying $5.00 a square for putting the siding on. Every time they would put on a square of shingles, I made $2.50 a square for finding, training, and supervising them. I was sometimes making $5.00 to $7.50 an hour while going to school.

So, one day I asked a banker I had met how to open a bank account. He replied, "What do you mean 'open a bank account'? Aren't you a football player at the junior college?"
I said, "Well, yeah, I am." Then I told him what I was doing.
He said, "You're incredible."

So, I opened an account and even began sending money home to my mother. I was hoping she could put the money down for a house and told her as much. Later it was more than upsetting to find out my stepdad had been using the money for himself. There was a lot of history with my stepdad, and most of it was not good. But that's another book entirely.

I was holding a job, attending Victoria Junior College on a football scholarship, making my grades, and supporting my mother. After I finished my two years of college in Victoria, I turned my job with Foreman Brothers over to someone else. For a college student, I had made a lot of money working for them. I guess I was always looking for unconventional ways to get things done and for ways to get ahead.

After I graduated from Victoria Junior college, several schools offered me football scholarships, including SMU, in Dallas. But Trinity University in San Antonio kept calling, wanting me to come there. The Trinity Tigers were a great football team at the time. They played some significant teams, including Ole Miss, Mississippi Southern, and Air Force Academy. I accepted their offer and went to Trinity, where I again was captain of the football team. I took pre-law and home-building--a double major. I lettered two years in football and two years in baseball before I graduated in 1960 with a Bachelor of Science degree.

Several of Trinity's best players went on to play in the National Football League. Two of them played for the San Francisco 49ers. Hank Schmidt was the biggest, fastest man I'd ever seen. He played left tackle, and I played left end. When a play began, Hank would take out both his man and mine as I ran down for a pass. He made me look good! I even received letters from the Green Bay Packers discussing my possible future in pro football. Then in one game, as I went up for a pass, a defensive back and a linebacker from the other team both hit me hard at the same time. I hit the ground and was not able to get up. My injury required surgery, where they removed my kneecap, scraped it, shaved it, and put it back on. So that pretty well ended my aspirations of becoming a professional football player. And that's why, when I graduated, I started working for Gold Bond in 1960.

It's funny how sometimes God is setting you up for the future, and you don't even know it. You're just living your life, doing your best, not knowing that your best and God's best are two different things entirely.

So the headline I saw in the Chronicle on my 42nd birthday, May 3, 1975, was not the kind of coverage I was used to getting. One month before that day, I wanted to try a new restaurant that opened in Louisiana, so we took the plane and went there for lunch. It was a far cry from being the dirty, snotty-nosed Jones kid who had no shoes growing up. My life was now everything most people aspired to be, and much of what I did was written up in either the society pages, the business section, or the sports section of the newspaper.

The article that day was the last thing I wanted to be reading. It reported that I was being forced to disband the Houston E-Z Riders because I hadn't come up with a $50,000.00 letter of credit by the league's arbitrary deadline. It mentioned the hurt and bitterness that was apparent as I talked about the situation at the Press Club the day before. It recounted how upset I was that the new owners had unexpectedly demanded a check from me. The World Team Tennis by-laws specifically exempted me from this letter of credit requirement. I had lost a few hundred thousand dollars on the team that previous year, but usually, that would not have been a problem for me. However, the bulk of my cash was tied up in my apartment projects. Since we were in the middle of a real estate recession in Houston, it was affecting all of us builders. I was working on a limited partnership for the team, and discussions were in process. There were several interested investors, with some well-known movie stars and celebrities among them, so I knew a cash influx for the team was coming in soon. But the league decided to set a quick deadline, and I was caught without resources right smack dab in the middle of it.

The very next day, the Sunday newspaper covered the story again. This time around, it included personal quotes from me and a lot of favorable commentary from the Chronicle staff writer about the league owners' unfair practices. But both articles stated that I was unable to post a $50,000 letter of credit. And that news was all it took for a few people to see an opportunity to make the most of my situation.

Nearly all of the big developers temporarily put their properties in Chapter 11 bankruptcy to weather the storm during the real estate recession. This legal action would prevent lenders and creditors from seizing or placing liens on their expensive assets during a short-term cash flow problem. I had not been in a position where I needed to do that, but the minute some negative news came out about the team, lenders descended like vultures. They wanted to call in their loans if I was even one month behind due to temporary cash flow issues. They were trying to swoop up my assets in any way possible.

I had an expert tax attorney at the time, but he was not a bankruptcy attorney. The moment I felt things slipping away, I asked him to please do whatever was needed to stop the losses. He went to a judge and said, "Judge, I don't know what I'm doing here. I need all the help I can get from you." Later, I met the judge who told me, "Mr. Jones, I know your name because I remember the day your attorney asked me for help, saying 'he didn't know what he was doing.' Right then and there, I knew that you'd end up losing everything because you didn't have the right attorney."

I asked my attorney to consult with other attorneys in Houston representing people with similar problems to mine. But he didn't do it. Unfortunately, I didn't realize that he hadn't done so until it was already too late.

In less than sixty days, I lost all my real estate, my hockey and tennis team ownership, the apartment projects, ice skating rinks, and nearly everything else I owned, all because I didn't have the right attorney. It was gone, all of it. I had nothing left. It all evaporated, even my eighteen-year marriage. Suddenly, all the stuff I had accumulated was also gone, and just as quickly, the life I was living came to an end. My hard-earned wealth, invested in real estate, apartment projects, ice-skating rinks, and sports franchises, came tumbling down like a stack of dominoes.

I had so little money that, for lunch, I'd go to Weingarten's, a grocery store located at the corner of Westheimer and Post Oak

Boulevard. In the deli, at the back, they had single servings of carrot and raisin salad for 35 cents. I had gone from eating expensive steaks at high-dollar restaurants in various cities to eating single servings of carrot and raisin salad. But I survived. Maybe that was because I was born and raised in a family that had so little. I was now alone at home waiting for the phone to ring, but nobody called. Most of the friends I was used to running with were nowhere to be found. I was not only broke; I was hundreds of thousands of dollars in debt. I felt like if I could stick my head in the sand like an ostrich and let a Mack truck run over me, that would be okay by me. It felt like my entire world had come to an end. My fall had not only been humiliating, but it had also been quite public, written about in articles and newspapers. I was mad at nearly everybody.

New Start and Good News

Several months later, an old friend of mine called and invited me to attend a meeting with him. He was a Lutheran. He told me about a men's meeting he wanted me to go to, and I agreed. It felt good just to have someplace to go and somebody to go with. He told me it was at the Marriott Hotel. We were a little bit late, but as we walked in, I noticed the tables had about 10 guys sitting around every one of them. On the wall, there was a sign with a Scripture that said, *His banner over me is love.* There were a lot of men at that meeting, called a Full Gospel Business Men's meeting. As a Presbyterian at the time, I had no idea what to expect. Frankly, it was nothing like what I was used to at my church.

One other thing, they were speaking in a language that I couldn't understand. I had never heard anyone speak in tongues and had no idea it was mentioned in several places in the Bible. I assumed one man who was speaking was from India and that the other person was interpreting for him. It was a good meeting, and the main speaker's testimony was quite interesting. But, as it ended, everyone stood and hugged each other. I thought to myself, wait a minute, we don't do this at our Presbyterian church. This kind of stuff doesn't seem quite right to me.

I soon learned that these were wonderful men who loved God. Norman Norwood, from my Gold Bond Building Materials days, saw me at one of the meetings and invited me to attend a Saturday meeting with him at a hotel downtown. We lived in the same subdivision and so he offered to pick me up. On the way, I discovered that Norman was the vice-president of the Full Gospel Business Men's Fellowship International. He worked closely with the founder and president of this world-wide organization, the late Demos Shakarian, an Armenian-American.

When we arrived, I was shocked to see around 1,000 people seated at tables. I was ushered to a seat toward the front of the room near the head table. On the raised platform stage, at least a few dozen men were sitting at a long table. The speaker that day was retired decorated fighter pilot, the late Colonel Heath "Bo" Bottomly, who served in the Pacific in World War II and later in Vietnam and Thailand. Upon retirement, he had become a Christian speaker, storyteller, writer, and coach. I still remember his story about chasing an enemy plane over the 38th parallel, which was expressly forbidden, because that pilot had been shooting at him. When Bottomly returned, he was court-martialed. I thought his telling of that story was phenomenal.

When he finished speaking, the Colonel said, "Does anyone here need to accept Jesus?"

I had accepted Jesus when I was a mere kid, and I thought that was all I needed to do. But I had certainly never lived my life for Him, not the way Colonel Bottomly had described. Even though I faithfully attended church, I didn't know anything about how to let Jesus guide me in my life, as he had described. So, I jumped up and ran to the front and re-dedicated my life to Jesus. From that day, my life began to change. I no longer attended church to be seen or because it was the right thing to do. I began to have a whole new relationship with Jesus.

I continued to attend Full Gospel Business Men's meetings. One night I was at home leisurely watching a Houston Rockets and Denver Nuggets basketball game. When the game ended, immediately, another television broadcast came on. It was a preacher I'd never heard of, named Kenneth Hagin. Pastor Hagin showed photos of two ladies who had come to him for healing prayer. Although each of them was lovely, they both had severely deformed legs. He prayed for them, and when he did, they were both healed instantly. I thought, "Well, that's good. But he's telling us this story to get us to send him a donation." I questioned his motive.

The person who came on next was an elderly farmer. He told about how God had helped him get his crops in when nothing else had worked. I thought to myself, "Whoa, farmers don't lie. I've been there, and they don't lie!" I began to listen intently. When the program ended, something strange happened.

My teenage son Clif, who was staying with me at the time, was asleep in the front bedroom. Dr. Swenson, then chief-of-staff at Bellaire General Hospital, was my next-door neighbor to one side; a renowned brain surgeon lived on the other side.

I had barely walked into my bedroom closet to take off my tennis shorts when my hands shot straight up into the air, and out of my mouth came sounds unlike any I'd ever heard. They weren't English. They were unnatural to me and yet felt supernatural. These utterances continued for some time. I quickly closed the bedroom door, returned to the closet, and closed the closet door. I knew if I were to have awakened my son, he would have panicked, never having heard about speaking in tongues. He would have run to get the doctors next door, and they would've transferred me to "the funny farm" in Austin by morning. All I know is that it felt like the anger and blame inside me were gone! It was as if a big dump truck had scooped it up, and I felt so much lighter, and I felt so free. It was really amazing!

The next day was Sunday, so I went, as usual, to my Presbyterian church, where I arrived early. I began to tell some of them about my experience the night before. They were looking at me with that "what-on-earth-are-you-talking-about look" on their faces.

I knew that I'd experienced what Scripture refers to as "the baptism of the Holy Spirit," but I could tell they had no idea what I was describing.

At another FGBMFI meeting, a guy from Louisiana who worked for a petroleum company gave an incredible testimony. He said, "I was at this place, and God told me to go down the street and over a block, and there would be a guy over there, and I went, and there was a guy, having a heart attack." I thought he had to be joking. God *told* him to go somewhere? Then a little bit later, he said, "God told me to go to this one place and…" Again, I thought he had to be joking. God had never spoken to me or told me where to go. I thought to myself, "I don't hear God telling me to go anyplace. I don't hear anything from Him at all!"

When the meeting closed, the speaker said to the crowd, "Friends, these men sitting here will be available to pray for you and any needs you may have." I immediately thought, "Oh, not me, Lord. You know that I don't know anything about how to do that." So, I just sat there, hoping to be invisible. A few seconds later, a little gray-headed gentleman walked over to me, stuck his finger in my face, and said sternly, "Young man, my wife wants you to come over here and pray for her." I slowly walked to where she was waiting, thinking, "Lord, I don't know how to pray for her. You know I've never prayed for anyone before." I then prayed, but honestly can't remember a thing I said.

When I finished, I noticed someone I knew, and I began walking toward them. However, as I did, a well-dressed man coming from the back of the ballroom walked up to me. He said, "Young man, God told me to tell you that you're going to be laying hands on people around the world, and they will be healed in the name of Jesus." I thought, What? God has never phoned to tell me anything like this before.

Full Gospel Business Men's Fellowship had a weekly television program each Sunday night called "Good News." People could call in for prayer during and after the broadcast. They used volunteers to answer the calls, and I had volunteered to help and on Sunday nights. The night following the FGBMFI meeting, I drove to the place where the volunteers answered the prayer line's phones. While driving to the call center, I heard an audible voice say, "When you get there, look at Matthew 10:1." I had a tape recorder on the front seat and checked to see if it was on. It wasn't. I felt the knobs on the car radio to make sure they were off. They were. I swept my arm back and forth behind the front seat to make sure nobody was in the back seat. There was nobody.

When I arrived, I opened my Bible and turned to Matthew 10:1. It said, "And when He had called His twelve disciples to Him, He gave them power over unclean spirits, to cast them out, and to heal all kinds of sickness and all kinds of disease."

I'd been there before to answer phones, but never had I been asked to pray for someone who was sick. I usually prayed for people with personal, relational, or financial problems. I was comfortable doing that because I was going through that myself. But I wasn't experienced at praying for sick people. We followed guides in our cubicles with Scriptures for prayers listed by topic to help us know how to pray for most things.

Wouldn't you know, the very first call I took was from a lady who said, "My name is Mrs. Nash. I would like for you to pray for me for healing because I have cancer."

When she mentioned "prayer for healing from cancer," I frantically began to search the prayer guide for some direction. Suddenly, Mrs. Nash said, "Excuse me, sir. Are you still there?" I answered, "Oh, yes ma'am, I'm here." At that point, I began to pray. I have no idea what I said or how I prayed. After all, I'd never prayed for someone with anything like that before.

They told me not very long after that, the woman called back to the "Good News" program to let everyone know that she had been healed of cancer.

During the summer of 1977, they took up an offering at one of the Full Gospel Business Men's meetings. I wanted to give so badly, but I had no money. Then I remembered that I still owned one large lot and one small one in Rockport, Texas. They were the very last things I owned. So, I wrote a note and placed it in the offering receptacle. It said, "I don't have any money, but I want to give. I am giving these lots in Rockport, Texas tonight in this offering."

When the meeting was over, Norman Norwood came to me and said, "E.Z., you may need these lots to get started again."
I replied, "No, Norman, all I need to get started again is Jesus."
And I meant it.
Then I transferred the titles for that property to the FGBMFI, and I'm sure they put the money to good use.

A young man was there that night who had just moved to Houston from Indiana. He had a phenomenal tenor singing voice. The Metropolitan Opera had come down to interview singers, and they interviewed him. His name was Jeoff Benward.
One of the Metropolitan Opera representatives asked Jeoff, "Who was your teacher? Who taught you to sing like this?"
Jeoff said, "Jesus."
They asked again, "No, no. Who was your teacher?"
Jeoff replied, "I've never had a voice lesson in my life. The only way I've learned to sing was by singing for Jesus."
To his credit, Jeoff turned down their offer to sing with the opera. He had no interest in singing for them. He was committed to singing for Jesus.

I met Jeoff at the event that night and learned that he and his family were looking for a place to live. I had a house, which was pretty empty. I said, "Jeoff, you can come live with me until you find a place of your own."

So Jeoff and his wife Candice, along with their young son Aaron, moved in with me. He began to accompany me as I went out to speak at meetings. He would sing and was always remarkably powerful and anointed! People really enjoyed Jeoff's music back then, and they still do today.

One night that same summer, Joe Poppell, a healing evangelist, ministered at Norman Norwood's house. He prayed for my severely painful knee and proclaimed what God's Word says about healing. My knee would often swell so badly my pant leg would be tight. That night, as he calmly prayed, I felt what seemed like a 22-rifle shot through my knee. After a few weeks, I could walk, run, and jog again without pain. It was a miracle. I had another astounding thing to add to my testimony, which I was starting to share.

A month or so later, I received a call from Mickie Winborn. Mickie, an internationally-known Bible teacher, taught weekly Bible studies for women at Tannie and Mary Teresa Pizzitola's home. Many Italian women from Catholic backgrounds were getting saved and filled with the Holy Spirit. The group decided to have an evening meeting so their husbands and male friends could attend. Mickie invited me to come and speak for that meeting, and I accepted. I had begun receiving several speaking invitations by then. I loved to tell people how even though I had lost all my money, I had now found true riches in Jesus Christ.

I was disappointed, however, when she called back a little later and said, "I'm so sorry, E.Z., but I must cancel my invitation for you to speak. The people we'd hoped to invite won't be able to come." They had invited a group of Italian men, but there was a boxing match that night, and they were all going to be watching it. So wisely, she postponed it until the following week.

When I arrived at the Pizzitola home on the designated night, I went in and began to meet people. They had moved their furniture around and had seating in their den set up in rows like a church. I walked over and laid my Bible on the mantel above the fireplace, then turned around. My eyes were drawn immediately to a beautiful young lady sitting in the middle of the room. Suddenly, the Lord spoke to me and said, "She's going to be your wife."

I said, "No, no, no!" I was certainly not looking for a wife and was trying to get my life put back together.

Later, when the meeting was over, I walked across the room to tell Mr. and Mrs. Pizzitola how much I appreciated the opportunity to share my testimony. I interrupted them as they were busy cleaning up and putting the chairs away. In a casual tone, I said to Mrs. Pizzitola, "There's one more thing. The Lord pointed out one young lady who was in the middle of the room and said, 'She's going to be your wife.'"
She said, "Oh? Who was that?" And I said, "I don't know who she is."
I identified her to them by explaining what she was wearing, and they said, "Oh, that's our daughter."
Embarrassed, I said, "Well, uh, excuse me, I have to go. I've got some things to do." So, I left.
The next day I called Mrs. Pizzitola and told her some things I felt the Lord had said to me about her daughter.
She said, "Okay, let me get back to you."

Then she called Lena (her daughter) and told her what I'd said. It was a few things the Lord said to me that I couldn't possibly naturally know. That's how Lena and I got acquainted and how I had another visit with her. Right after that, I saw her at a home prayer meeting, and the next thing you know, I'd fallen head over heels in love with her. She had such a great personality and was as beautiful on the inside as she was on the outside. The same year I re-dedicated my life to Jesus, she was born again while attending Mickie Winborn's women's Bible study. Both of us had similar experiences when we were baptized in the Holy Spirit, and we were both committed to serving God with all of our hearts. I was 44 years old, and she was only 25. She had a 7-year-old son, Paul Michael, who she was raising on her own. Even though there was a nineteen-year age difference between us, and I was flat broke and deeply in debt, when I asked her to marry me, she said yes. Some sarcastic friends later told me that's actually quite a miracle in itself!

Marriage, Ministry and Miracles

Lena and I were making plans to get married, but she wasn't buying anything new for our wedding day, mostly because I was so broke. Mickie Winborn, her spiritual mother, soon found out about this. "Oh no!" she said. "You ARE going to have a new dress!" And she bought the dress Lena wore when we got married on the eighth of April in 1978.

Our friend Jeoff Benward was the best man, and his wife was matron of honor. The two of us stood with the officiating minister and some of our family members under a gazebo on the courthouse lawn at Cold Springs, Texas. Lena's son Paul Michael and Aaron Benward, Jeoff's son, leaned over the gazebo rails and chewed on their bubble gum. There was a county fair going on that day in Cold Springs, and some other Christian friends of ours were singing as part of the program. But when Jeoff began to sing acapella for our wedding ceremony, a crowd started to gather. His perfect voice resounding across the courthouse lawn, people kept walking in our direction, and we ended up having quite a large number of people. Years later, people would come up to us and say, "We were there when y'all got married!"

Since I had no money to pay for a honeymoon, an old friend of mine who owned the Waterwood Resort near Conroe, gave us free accommodations and meals for a few nights. It was a far cry from what I had been used to just a few years earlier, but I felt like the richest man in the world with my wife by my side.

Once we were married, Lena traveled with me when I went to speak at different places. One of those places was San Antonio. Lena and our seven-year-old son Paul Michael went with me. God worked it out so that soon after our marriage, I legally adopted Lena's young son, and I raised him as my own.

There were several nuns at the meeting that night in San Antonio. As I prayed for those nuns, they would often "fall out" under the power of the Holy Spirit. There were "catchers" standing by to lower them softly and safely to the floor. Seeing that, Paul Michael turned to Lena and said, "Mom, I want to be one of Daddy's catchers.'" Of course, he wasn't big enough to do that, but he was willing and wanted to be involved.

I continued to receive ministry invitations, and one was to minister in Lawton, Oklahoma, on Memorial Day weekend. Lawton is the home of the U.S. Army's Fort Bliss. It was somewhat confusing at the hotel because the folks from the military base were having a celebration there that night, auctioning liquor by the bottle. At the very same time, our meeting was in the next room.

When we arrived, our room was almost empty. Hardly anyone was there. Our host, clearly disappointed with the turnout, walked up and said, "Well, you know, this is Memorial Day weekend. The size of the crowd is often determined by how well-known the speaker is. It requires a lot to get people out these days."

His negativity didn't bother me a bit. I paid very little attention to what he was saying, and soon, people began to arrive from all over. Some had driven from little towns that were twenty to thirty miles away. Before long, the place was packed.

As I gave my testimony that night, I couldn't keep my eyes off a certain gentleman. It was apparent he was a pretty tough guy. I later learned that he was a coach from Lawton Junior College. Some people, who recognized him, seemed to wonder what he was doing at a Christian event. But God just kept pointing him out to me.

When I began to pray for the people, some would fall out in the Spirit. God healed some people and gave me many words of knowledge for others.

Finally, I asked the coach point-blank, "Sir, you don't believe me, do you?"

He said, "No."

I said, "Well, okay."

Then the Lord told me, "Tell him to stand up."

So, I said to the man, "Excuse me, sir, would you please stand up?"

As he stood, I pointed my hand in his direction, and God hit him. I mean, really hit him. He crumpled and fell to the floor. He was dizzy, but the people were amazed. It was as if they couldn't believe what they were seeing.

When he got back up, I asked him, "You still don't believe me, do you?"

He replied, "Well, no, I don't."

I said, "God, touch him."

God touched him again and, down to the floor, he went. I asked, "Now, do you believe me?"

He said, "Well, I believe so. I think so."

The good news is that he and quite a few others were born again that night. That was one of the meetings that I fondly remember where God did some amazing things. From there, our speaking invitations increased.

One Saturday night Jeoff Benward, Lena, and I drove down to Lake Jackson, Texas, south of Houston. The meeting was at the Holiday Inn. Unfortunately, the meeting in which I was to minister took up one side of the ballroom. Another group rented the other side, and it was a big noisy party.

As we walked in, I said, "Oh, Lord, not another one!" We began our meeting as planned. I asked Jeoff to sing. So, he started singing

The Lord's Prayer. As he sang, what had been a boisterous, noisy group on the other side suddenly grew quiet. You could've heard a pin drop over there. No one spoke a word. When Jeoff finished the song, the people at the party next door burst into thunderous applause.

One weekend, Lena and I drove to Dallas to speak at the invitation of a pastor friend of Norman Norwood's, the late Jim Hester. Jim had once been a Baptist pastor at a large church in Houston. However, he went to a family's home one night and was baptized in the Holy Spirit. Because of that experience, he was asked to leave the Baptist church. He moved to Dallas and planted a church, which grew quite large. He asked if I would come up and speak there.

I had received invitations to speak at several other places that same weekend: Friday night, Saturday morning and evening, and Sunday morning and evening. We were flat broke when we left home for Dallas. Frankly, we were anxious when we arrived, not knowing if our hosts were going to pay for the hotel accommodations. Saturday morning at breakfast, a man came over and gave us an envelope with $50.00 in it. That $50.00 was enough to pay for Friday night's hotel stay. We were quite relieved! It didn't only require faith to pray for people to be healed of their sicknesses and diseases. Sometimes, it required faith just to make it from meeting to meeting.

On Sunday morning, I was to speak at Pastor Hester's church. He teasingly called me, "James Garner." At that time, I often was mistaken for the actor. He had played the part of Maverick on the television series by that name. I did look like James Garner, although he was five years older than me. People would sometimes come up to me in public places and ask for an autograph. I would never sign, "James Garner," although a couple of times I did sign, "Maverick." Garner, whose real name was James Scott Bumgarner, was born in Norman, Oklahoma, not far from my birthplace.

Pastor Jim had reserved a hotel room for "James Garner" and asked that they give us a nice room. That night, when we climbed into bed, suddenly we felt something strange. What in the world was it? Our bed was full of rice! The hotel had not cleaned the room. We called room service, and they moved us to another room. We never knew what crazy surprises might await us, but we were serving the Lord, and we both loved it.

We had a good service at Jimmy Hester's church. He was a great pastor, and his people were enthusiastic and hungry for more of God. Those five times in three days were the most I'd ever spoken at one time. Folks will keep you busy if you are willing to do it. I was too new to have learned to pace myself. I wanted to do everything I could do for the Lord at that point. Now bear in mind, I was working full-time in real estate development along with my weekend traveling schedule.

Much to Lena's dismay, I had a dedicated practice of fasting three days before every speaking engagement. I really wanted to be able to tune in and hear from God, and I was convinced that fasting made a difference. She worried because when I had a meeting each weekend, I was not eating for three days of every single week. Yet, I was strong and healthy and didn't feel weakened by it, and the meetings were marked by the miraculous, so I wasn't concerned about missing a little food.

One of the FGBMI meetings I'll never forget was in the Ozarks. It was a three-day meeting with multiple speakers, of which I was one. I elected to be the last speaker because I didn't have the reputation the others had. So, as the meetings began, a few of the more well-known men spoke. The next day, others ministered, and I was going to be speaking on the last day.

There were several hundred men in attendance. It was at a beautiful place, and I was honored to be a speaker. As I heard those well-known men speak, they had great testimonies, and the people were very interested in what they had to say.

I thought, "I don't have much to say compared to the testimonies of these great men." They had lived through some incredible experiences. When I stood to speak, the Lord spoke to me. He drew my attention to a particular redheaded man and gave me words of knowledge concerning him.

I said, "Sir, you are married to an African-American woman." Then I began to share things about him, facts he knew I couldn't have possibly known in the natural. As I told him, he began to cry. Others attending were astounded that someone who had never met him could tell him such detailed things about himself and his wife. It expanded from there, and God gave me words of knowledge for every man in the room.

I don't think a man was there that night who didn't get a word of knowledge from the Lord. God did so much that we ministered far beyond the planned closing time. But even though it was late that night when we finished, not one person left the meeting. It's incredible what can happen when God is in control.

I simply shared the words of knowledge that God gave me. I did what He instructed me to do. I wanted only to glorify Him. As a result, God set those men on fire and sent them out doing good things. A pastor friend of mine, now deceased, was invited to speak at a nearby church about a month later. He told us that the people were still talking about all that happened the night I'd ministered. I received several invitations to speak as a result of what God had done. But it's of the utmost importance that you know it wasn't me, but it was God speaking. It wasn't my knowledge or ability. God was at work, and I only did what God told me and said what I heard Him say. I would never have known any of those things on my own. It was just as Jesus said, "… Very truly I tell you, the Son can do nothing by Himself; He can do only what He sees His Father doing, because whatever the Father does the Son also does." (John 5:19 NIV)

In 1979 I was invited to minister at an event in Atlanta, Texas, at their Civic Auditorium.

Lena and I drove up from Houston and arrived a little bit early. As we sat in the car, another car pulled up alongside ours. The driver got out of his car and walked around to the passenger side to open his wife's door. I thought *this guy is such a gentleman,* but then I understood why he had hurried over there.

His wife was crippled, with such twisted legs, she could barely walk. He pulled out her crutches and handed them to her, then helped her stand. At that moment, I heard the Lord say, "I'm going to heal her tonight." I didn't dare mention it to anyone else, but I told Lena.

They struggled to get over to the bottom of the steps that led into the auditorium, and I said, "I don't think she's going to be able to make that climb." To my surprise, though it was difficult, she made it. Her husband helped her down the aisle, and they sat on the front row.

The meeting began, and soon it was time for me to speak. Once I finished giving my testimony, I came down from the stage and began to pray for people. I worked my way through the group, calling out the words of knowledge God gave me. People responded, and the power of God was evident. One after another, I prayed for those needing healing. One distinguished black gentleman wanted prayer for a weakness in his arm and hand, a diagnosed condition. He said he didn't even have enough strength to hold a tennis racket, although he looked muscular and very fit. When I finished praying for him, before he turned to leave, he shook my hand. There was a remarkable new strength in his grip that surprised both of us. I could feel the level of faith in the room growing stronger. I ministered to two or three more who needed prayer. Then I knew it was time for me to pray for one person, someone who hadn't even asked for prayer. She was on the front row with her crutches beside her, the lady God had told me He was going to heal.

I walked over to her and said, "Ma'am, let me see your crutches." She gave them to me, and to her surprise, I handed them to someone on the other side of the room. Then I turned back to her and said, "Okay. Let's get up and walk." She looked at me as if to say, "Do what? You know I can't walk without my crutches!" I said, "Come on, stand up." She haltingly stood, and I grabbed onto her hand. I said, "Now walk, in the name of Jesus." She obviously had as little faith as I had when the Lord told me earlier that He would heal her.

"We can do this," I said. "Walk, in the name of Jesus." She stared at me in disbelief. I repeatedly told her to walk in Jesus' name. Soon, she took a stumbling step, and then another. Then three steps, followed by three more. I heard the bones in her knees and legs make a crackling sound. Before long, she was walking all around the auditorium. People were crazy with excitement and shouting with glee. Tears were running down the faces of men and women alike.

When I gave her the microphone, she and her husband explained that the church they attended was building a new facility. They had just poured the foundation and were going to dedicate it the following day. She told me that she was planning to go there and dance all over that floor, celebrating what God had done. I left that night reminded of Jesus' words in John 14:14, "If you ask anything in My name, I will do it."

Monumental Meetings and Men's Ministries

In 1979, an interdenominational event, spearheaded by some Catholic believers, was in the planning stages. It was the height of the charismatic renewal, and people from many denominations were receiving the baptism of the Holy Spirit. They asked me to serve on the steering committee and informed me the event would be at The Summit. The Summit is where the Houston Rockets played basketball, and it is now the home of Lakewood Church.

An interesting story related to this happened a few years earlier, in 1974, when I was an owner of the Houston Aeros hockey team. Irving Kaplan, who then owned the Houston Rockets NBA basketball team, led the effort to build this new arena called The Summit. But to accomplish that, Irving needed to own 51% of the Houston Aeros ice hockey team. Otherwise, they would put the Rockets somewhere else. But he couldn't seem to secure the necessary stock.

At the time, I held the controlling Aeros stock. I would have sold some stock to Irving, but it was the end of the year, and I couldn't. The other shareholders wouldn't sell him any stock, either, because of losing their tax advantages. So, even though it was risky, I loaned him the shares he needed to achieve 51% ownership. He and I had nothing in writing, only a gentleman's agreement, sealed with a handshake. Mr. Kaplan later returned the stock after the plans to build the Summit became finalized.

Years later, I would realize the significance of my loaning him the stock. You see, had I not provided that stock, the Summit, which the Houston Rockets would call home for 29 years, and which later became home to Lakewood Church, would never have been built!

So when I was on the steering committee for Jesus '79, it was then that I realized that my stock loan five years earlier, in another season of my life entirely, had helped build it. The event drew approximately 12,000 people. Mother Angelica, a well-known spirit-filled Catholic, was one of the invited speakers. Ben Kinchlow, renowned author, television personality, and host of The 700 Club, was also one of our guest ministers. It was a full day of praise and worship and speakers and prayer for unity.

None of us at the time knew that the Summit would one day become Lakewood Church.

We followed up the next two years with Jesus '80 and Jesus '81. I was honored to serve on the executive committee for each of those meetings. Many of the great relationships I forged while working with Christian businesspeople and pastors in our city lasted for decades. These gatherings were so inspiring and were well worth the effort we put into them. Many people came to the Lord, and lives were forever changed as attendees responded to the altar calls at these events.

In 1981 I launched an interdenominational men's ministry called Luv Ya Houston. The name was patterned after a sports slogan in our city at the time. It was for Houston's businessmen, and we met at noon-time for lunch at various locations. At one point, I was having a meeting somewhere in the city every Monday, Wednesday, and Friday. Each gathering consisted of fellowship, Christian singers, and speakers. For a time, meetings were held at a restaurant bar, then later at Wyatt's Cafeteria in their private party room. Then we met at Marathon Towers private dining room and various Houston hotel restaurants for more than sixteen years. I hauled the equipment, speakers, tripod stands, wires, and microphones in my car to each of those meetings. Thousands of men attended over that span of years, and untold numbers of men received Jesus in their lives. Many were baptized in the Holy Spirit, prayed for, and ministered to. We also helped provide support for countless ministries since we took offerings at every meeting, but I did not receive a penny. We supported missionaries, blessed guest ministers who spoke, helped feed the poor and adopted families at Christmas. We provided turkeys at Thanksgiving to churches all across Houston, so they could help those in need. Putting on Christian concerts and holding food giveaways in inner-city neighborhoods, our mission was to be the hands of Jesus to those around us. Our motto was "to lend a helping hand."

One day, while I was working out at the Westwood Racquet Ball Club with my friend, Tom DeLay, I overheard two young men talking about the Lord. I leaned over and said, "Who are y'all talking about?"
One said, "Jesus," and I said, "Oh, who's he?"
I was pulling his leg, but then he asked, "What's your name?"
I said, "I'm E.Z. Jones."
The other young man, who worked at KSBJ, said, "Oh my gosh, he's on our board!"

I found out that the young man who initially asked my name was Doug. He was passionate about the Lord and compassionate about needy people. Little did I know that God would one day raise him up to lead on an international ministry level. With his beautiful wife Lisa, and daughter Ashley, Doug Stringer now ministers in nations around the world via their Somebody Cares America/International ministry.

Doug came to our Luv Ya Houston meetings, where he met other Christian businessmen. When they discovered that he ministered to the homeless in the Montrose area, they began to donate various things to support him. One time someone gave Luv Ya Houston a car; I then gave it to Doug. Someone donated a house along with the equity in it, and I then gave it to Doug. Some of his team lived in that house for a while.

Another young man came to our meetings who was in The Inner City Boyz. This group did rap music to promote the gospel among inner-city kids, and they were reaching kids by the hundreds. When they helped guys get off drugs and get their lives turned around, I found someone to donate bedding and mattresses for them. In his early years, I felt fatherly toward Doug, and back then, The Inner City Boyz called me their white daddy.

For years, I used my business, ministry, and personal connections to bless, equip and launch new ministries. Like a Barnabas, I'd been able to open doors for those who had no connections themselves. I later received a prophetic word to that effect, and only then did it hit me how much God had used me in that way. I had no dad to help me as I grew up. There was nobody around to give me anything and no one to even offer advice. How I loved helping younger people with what they were passionate about, especially when they were passionate about the Lord.

In 1983, I was invited to give my testimony on TBN's Praise the Lord program based out of California, and a year later, I was also asked to be a guest on The 700 Club, the program launched by Pat Robertson's CBN network. On each network, after sharing my life story, I began to call out words of knowledge about various conditions people had. Both times, calls with praise reports of healings started coming in from all over the country. It was exciting but also scared me a little. I didn't want my ego to get the best of me as it had done in the past.

A major recession hit the oil industry in the United States in 1983 and '84, and Houston was especially hard hit. Thousands of businesses in the city were affected, and many of their employees were devastated. Petroleum engineers, geologists, and others connected to oil companies were losing their jobs. To help these newly unemployed men, I had an idea. Under the umbrella of Luv Ya Houston, we launched a free service called "Job Search" on Christian radio station KSBJ. After getting air time donated so that we could advertise what we were doing, things took off.

Although it appeared to listeners that we had a large staff, it was only Lena and me. We worked from our home, matching resumes men sent in with job openings that companies reported to us. We felt compelled to do that because so many families were suffering financially due to their new unemployment status. Worse still, marriages were falling apart, and children were being affected. So we served the unemployed as diligently as we could.

People being people, some who were suffering financially, would become impatient and angry. They'd yell, "Why haven't you found me a job yet?" Ours was a free service, but they didn't realize it was just the two of us matching job openings with personnel on our living room floor out of hearts of love. But it was gratifying when we succeeded and saw the difference our efforts could make in the life of a family.

Around that same time, I was partnering with a Christian businessman I knew, and we were building apartment projects. This allowed me to provide a rent-free apartment for Doug Stringer. Doug had started Turning Point Ministries and was doing street ministry in Montrose and other areas around the city. He was both generous and hospitable and had a heart to disciple those in need. It wasn't uncommon to see homeless guys sleeping all over the floor in that apartment. Lena soon realized that they didn't have enough food and began to take groceries to them regularly. We have a lot of stories from those days, and some are pretty funny. Others are just eye-opening, like when we gave a couple of the homeless guys some money (to help them out) and told them they could do odd jobs for us. We found out our funds were used for liquor and prostitutes, learning quickly that all cash "gifts" for his homeless crew needed Doug's oversight.

There is a young man named Jay who has attended our church now for several years. When his father came to visit one Sunday, his dad said, "Oh my gosh, son! I know your pastor!" E.Z. Jones and his wife Lena bought groceries for us when I was homeless and lived with Doug Stringer. Don't you ever leave Pastor E.Z. because he's a good man." We never know the ripple effect our actions will have, sometimes even through the generations.

It was also in 1983 that I received a prophetic warning. I now realize I didn't heed it very well. Betty Jo Frank, a pastor's wife from Rosenberg, Texas, prophesied to me at a meeting I attended. We had never met, and she said,

> *"I see you have many anointings. But don't stray too far from your greatest anointing. And that's healing the sick. I see you getting pictures and words of knowledge and laying hands on the sick. You have great compassion for those in need of healing, and I see you praying for people, and the sick are getting well! You are laying hands on people, and they're being healed in the name of Jesus. So don't get distracted and don't neglect your greatest anointing."*

But I was busy with Luv Ya Houston and the citywide events, so the healing ministry took a back seat. In retrospect, I realize that the enemy, always a liar, put a subtle fear in me that I might become prideful because of the healing ministry. I had been prideful when I became successful in business. Since I didn't want that to happen again, I listened to the enemy's lie instead of the word I received.

By 1984, Luv Ya Houston was thriving, and attendance was in the hundreds. Edwin Louis Cole, a well-known spiritual father figure and author/speaker, wanted to conduct a significant event in our city. Someone gave him my name, saying, "If you want to put something on in Houston, you need to see this man." It wasn't long before Ed Cole asked me to chair his National Christian Men's Event. It would be at Hofheinz Pavilion, a 7,100-seat multi-purpose arena on the University of Houston campus in Houston. I told him that Luv Ya Houston would do it, which meant that most of the work fell on me. I worked hard to see the event succeed. Some of our Luv Ya Houston guys helped me distribute brochures and various other things, but all the legwork and networking was up to me. The members of our board were servant-hearted, but some owned companies and ran organizations. Others were market partners in major restaurants or entrepreneurs, so they did what they could, but their time was quite limited. Volunteering at the noon-time Luv Ya Houston meetings was all some of them could spare in their busy week.

In the end, Hofheinz Pavilion was packed. The newspapers said 7800 men attended since it was standing room only. It was the largest attended Christian men's rally since World War II, and it was a precursor to Promise Keepers, the evangelical ministry for men that numbered in the hundreds of thousands several years later. After that, many well-known leaders came asking me to coordinate their meetings. Josh McDowell, the famous Christian author, walked into my office one day, laid all of his books on my desk, and said, "Hey, I'd like for you to help put on some meetings for me." But I told him, "No, that's not what I'm supposed to be doing."

In a way, it was all very heady, but it was pulling me away from the healing ministry.

Then Robert Gonzalez launched Christian radio station KSBJ, and it went on air in the '80s. I served on the board with several wonderful men. It was awesome to work alongside Lakewood's founding pastor, the late John Osteen, an amazing man who was a fiery preacher loved by people far and wide. He was humorous and quick-witted and his wife Dodie has always been one of the most caring and genuine people I've ever met. One time, she was having lunch with her daughter Tamara at a restaurant called Taste of Texas. Across the room, I was walking to the salad bar and her daughter said to her, "Mom, that looks like James Garner over there." Once I turned and started walking in their direction where Dodie could see me, she said to Tamara, "Honey, that's not James Garner, that's E.Z. Jones." And she quickly invited me over to their table and gave me a hug and introduced me to her daughter.

Some others on the KSBJ board included the long-time pastor of Braeswood Assembly of God, the late Earl Banning as well as the late Pastor John Bisagno of First Baptist Church and Pastor Ed Young, Sr. of Second Baptist Church. These were all such well-respected and dedicated men and I enjoyed an interdenominational circle of friends that I loved very much. We experienced a lot of unity and churches worked together back then to accomplish things across the city. Because of my extensive business background, I was considered a liaison between the pastors and the business community.

By New Year's Eve of 1989, Lena and I attended Betty Jo and Gene Frank's Church of Living Waters in Rosenberg. A special speaker named Dale Gentry was coming to speak who was known for his prophetic gifting. Lena wanted to go, so I relented. "Okay, I'm going," I told her, "But I will sit behind the biggest man there. I don't need another prophetic word. Every place I go, I get a word."

At the end of his message, he began to call people out in the congregation to prophesy over them. Dale pointed at Lena and asked, "Ma'am, is that your husband sitting there. The one who is behind that post?" She nodded. Then he said,

> *"Sir, God's going to take you down another path. I see that you two are going to go through the death of a vision. Things in days past that you thought were going to happen--you will die to them. God has given you a pioneering gift. That means you will give birth to something. I see a day coming. I don't know when, that a man of God is going to lay hands on both of you and you're going to go into full-time ministry. I don't know if that means a church, a work, or a fellowship. But it's a birthing gift that brings forth fresh life, fresh anointing."*

He continued,

> *"God is going to give you favor with non-traditional people. There will be signs and wonders from the laying on of your hands. There will be emotional and physical healings and miracles and a simple faith walk. You will have to trust the Holy Spirit and lean not on your own understanding. But there will be a heavy anointing."*

We were dumbfounded! We had never thought we'd be ordained or ever be in full-time ministry. We'd assumed at that point that we would continue to earn our living in the business world and minister "on the side." We didn't know what this ministry he spoke of was going to look like or what we would even be doing. "Full-time ministry to non-traditional people." What could that possibly mean? I felt sure we wouldn't be called to pastor a church. It seemed to me that there were already enough churches.

God began dealing with us about ministry, and in 1990, our time of transition arrived. My real estate brokerage was failing, no matter how much I tried to keep it afloat. Later that year we sold our home, which was our only asset, and we paid off every debt we had. We also sold most of our furniture and many of our household goods. We were now without a business, and we had no place to live. In fact, we didn't even have an address. The few possessions we had left after the sale of our home were in storage, and we were living with what we needed packed neatly inside the trunk of our car.

We were unencumbered and surrendering fully to "the call of God," although we didn't know where He would send us or what He wanted us to do. Paul Michael was 20 by then, and we told God that we'd go anywhere if He would just show us. Since we had friends living in various cities in the U.S., we decided this would be our chance to go different places and ask, "God, is this where You want our ministry to begin?"

First, we drove to a friend's house in West Palm Beach, Florida. We loved staying with our long-time friend Dan Lassetter, who had a condo right on the beach. For three weeks, we enjoyed Florida. God didn't say a word to us during this time.

Next, we went to Pennsylvania, where we stayed for three weeks with some other friends, Tom and Peggy Covert. Tom worked as an executive with an oil company and had gotten saved at one of my Luv Ya Houston meetings several years prior. He and his wife were very hospitable, and they lived in an elegant historic home in Warren, Pennsylvania. Peggy was a superb cook, and we enjoyed delicious home-cooked meals during our entire three-week stay. But again, God didn't say a word.

We had ten days of speaking engagements scheduled in Leesburg, Virginia, near Washington, D.C. So, we left Pennsylvania for Leesburg. While in the D.C. area, we experienced some remarkable meetings, and God did some amazing things. But one thing He didn't do was to tell us where we were supposed to live and what we were supposed to be doing.

On our way back to Houston, we stopped in Tulsa and attended some church meetings. Then we went to a powerful three-day conference in Broken Arrow, Oklahoma. My sister Faye had given me and Lena one of her home-cooked pecan pies when we drove through Springdale, Arkansas, on the way there. We carefully set it on top of the microwave in our hotel room. The second day, we noticed that a large piece was missing, and a trail of crumbs was going from the microwave to the door. The housekeeper must have been hungry and just decided to help herself. We laughed about this for days. But, once again, there was nothing there for us.

Back in Houston, where we had begun our journey several weeks earlier, we temporarily stayed with Lena's mom and dad at their home. After six weeks had passed and we still hadn't found a place to live, Lena was discouraged, and she said, "Let's go drive down our old street and look at our house." She was referring to the one we had sold. It had been our home since we were married in 1978, and we had never lived anywhere else as a couple.

So, we drove down the street on which we had lived. As we did, there were two small patio homes for lease, down one block and across the street, from our old house. We stopped and looked at them. One of them was very dirty. Lena is a bit of a clean freak--well, more than a bit! We were shocked when God woke her up later in the middle of the night and told her, to her surprise, that we were to lease the dirty one.

We said yes to God and leased it from the landlord. Lena's entire family worked on that house for a week, cleaning and scrubbing it until she loved the end result. While it was half the size of our former home, it was affordable to rent. We thought we'd be there one year only, but as it turned out, we ended up living in that rented patio home for nearly nineteen years. But at that point, we still didn't know where God wanted us to do ministry or in what capacity He desired to use us.

It was a rough few years of transition as we waited on the word of the Lord. Because it just so happened that all of the speaking engagements that previously kept us so busy had somehow vanished. No one asked us to speak or minister, and we rarely even got calls to pray for anybody. It's as if all of a sudden, after saying yes to full-time ministry, no one needed us to do any ministry, of any kind, anywhere!

One night in 1993, we visited a group of friends at Paul and Kathleen Keese's home in Sugar Land. The late Lenny Weston was visiting from Ohio. Lenny had at one time been on the pastoral staff of a church we'd attended years earlier. It was a night of fun and fellowship until we began to worship. As we did, a heavy anointing fell in the room, and Pastor Lenny began to prophesy. He looked across the room at the two of us, and his voice thundered as he said,

> *"No longer will YOU say what you will and will not do! No longer will YOU say what you will and will not be!"*

He said several other things that we were too stunned to make sense of, but there was no mistaking that God was all over it. As we were talking with a few of the others there later that night, we innocently recalled, "The only thing we have always said is that we would never be pastors. Neither of us feels qualified to pastor a church."

The next day people began asking us if we'd like to start some meetings. We told them, "No." They insisted, "If you do, we want to come."

We explained emphatically, "Thank you, but we aren't going to be having any meetings."

A few days later, Lenny talked to us some more about the word he had given us and what he thought it meant. Then Paul and Kathleen, in whose home we had received the word, said, "Let's just start some meetings in our home." We relented and started meeting there on Thursday nights, and the Holy Spirit moved significantly. We experienced words of knowledge, and other gifts of the Holy Spirit were flowing freely, and the Lord's presence was so strong that soon, without realizing it, we had become a church.

In June of that year, we were ordained into the ministry, exactly as Dale Gentry had prophesied four years earlier. At that point, we began holding Sunday morning services.

A guy who was the worship leader at another church would drop by and lead worship for us. Then he had to quickly pack up so he wouldn't be late to lead worship at his regular church.

It was 1993, and I was 60 years old.

Most men my age were focused on retiring. Me? I was planting a church. We had sold everything we owned and were living off the equity from the sale of our home. The balance had greatly diminished because we had been trying for more than two years to find out what God wanted us to do. And we had no income of any kind during this time. A friend I had known since the '80s named Clay Hill called out of the blue one day, asking how much money it took for me and Lena to live each month. I told him, and he said, "I'll give you half that amount as long as the Lord tells me to." He sent us a check for half of our living expenses for more than a year and a half. The month he called to say he was no longer going to be sending the check was the same month fifteen guys from Luv Ya Houston each pledged $100 each to help with my support. It was the first time I accepted a penny in all the years I had been doing the Luv Ya Houston meetings. Clay sure heard from God as we could not have made it through that time without his help, and it was amazing to us how he knew exactly when to stop. God was proving that He would be faithful, and we were learning to trust Him in ways that were new for us.

By 1994, we had a church membership of 40-50 people. So, we moved our church services to an elementary school. Our church was called The Shepherd's Church. Later, we changed the name to The Epicenter. The mission of our church was to equip people to do the work of the ministry and to develop fivefold ministers (pastors, evangelists, apostles, teachers, and prophets), as mentioned in Ephesians 4:11. There was a strong emphasis on praise and worship, and the tangible presence of God was usually in the room. We had faith for healing, both physical and emotional, and we wanted to teach people to be sensitive to the Spirit of God.

A dear friend of ours was a great Bible teacher, and he and his wife were assisting us in our new church plant. He encouraged us to start home groups to better disciple the people. Having home cell groups wasn't in Lena's and my heart, but we didn't exactly know what we were doing, so we decided to allow him to cast the vision. We launched cell groups, and after three weeks, virtually everyone quit coming. It looked like our new church had disintegrated before our very eyes. We were heartsick. We felt like, "Okay, we failed. Being pastors wasn't it."

It was a difficult time, but what was funny was that on Sundays, many who'd been attending our church would call and ask, "Where are you and Lena going to attend church?" They said, "We want to come with you." So, for a while, we headed something that must've looked like a roving band that visited one church after another. Soon, it seemed like they all wanted us to relaunch our church. So after about three months, we began again in another home, but without the cell groups.

The vision in our hearts remained to develop five-fold ministers and to experience God's presence in praise and worship. New people began to attend, and we quickly outgrew the home where we were meeting. We moved our services to a room at the Aerodrome Ice Skating Rink. That was where the minor ice hockey team, the AHL Houston Aeros, practiced. Their coach was Terry Ruskowski, an Aeros player when I was one of the original WHA Houston Aeros team owners. With Terry on our team, we had won two world championships. Now, with Terry's help, we procured a place for our Sunday services.

We had some colorful members at those meetings at the Ice Rink. Coach Ken Hatfield was then head coach of the Rice Owls, Rice University's NCAA football team. Coach Ken and his wife attended. His wife was a barrel racer, someone who rides a horse around barrels in an arena. Another couple who was attending also had a barrel racing horse. They called him "Old Buck." Buck wasn't running very well, so the wife asked, "Have you ever prayed for a horse?"
I said, "Well, ma'am, I don't know that I have."
She asked, "Well, would you come out and pray for mine?"
I agreed to pray for Old Buck.

Sure enough, God healed Old Buck, and he began winning races. Maybe it was because I had taken an interest and had prayed for him, but Buck started tithing. Well, I guess I should say his owner, who went to our church, tithed off his winnings. At one point, we had a total of seven barrel racers attending our church. The owners were asking me to pray that their horses would win. It was an exciting time for our new members and everybody came to church with lots of anticipation.

The space at the Ice Rink was limited. It served us well until one day, out of the blue, we received a notification. Due to renovations, our church would no longer be able to conduct services at the Aerodrome. We had only one week to move out, which meant we needed to find another place fast.

A week is not a long time, so Lena and I began a quick search for a new church location the following morning. We drove around Sugar Land looking for an appropriate rental space. Because of my many years in business, I knew tons of business owners in the area. A few of them, hearing we were looking for a place for our Sunday morning services, began to offer their spaces since they were not open on Sundays. We checked out a few. Lena, who is quite discerning, didn't feel they were right for us. I was growing desperate and a little impatient with her lack of enthusiasm for these spaces. Time was running out, and finding a new meeting place was beginning to seem impossible.

Then Lena felt we should look in the shopping center a half block from our patio home. Buster Freedman of United Equities owned and managed properties all over Texas. It just so happened to be one of his centers. On the way, I assured her there would be no rental space in that shopping center. Besides, I knew that Buster would never rent space to a church. After all, I was a former real estate developer, and I had talked to him about it once before. She still insisted. When we pulled into the shopping center parking lot, Lena felt we should go to the opposite end. Sure enough, there WAS a space for rent. I'd somehow missed it. We exited the car and walked up to the door. Lena reached out and put her hand on the window, smiled, and looked up to me, and said, "E.Z., this is it. This is our space!"

Since she was so sure, I called Buster's office for an appointment, even though it seemed pointless. I decided to "play my ace in the hole." Remember how we got access to the Aerodrome? It was because of the help of my good friend, NHL star, and then Houston Aeros coach, Terry Ruskowski. Terry was the only professional player in history to serve as captain on four teams and he was a spiritual son to me. I knew that Buster Freedman's Vice-President of leasing, Tim Sandifer, was a serious hockey fan. So Terry and I, with an armload of hockey memorabilia, went to see him. To say that he was impressed would be an understatement. God was all over that meeting.

While they had never rented to a church before, and never have since, they gave us a six-month lease at a deeply reduced price. Plus, they waived the standard requirement of us paying our common share of taxes, maintenance, and insurance that owners incur each year. God had indeed spoken to Lena. It was a divine appointment. But now, we had to focus on building out our new space. And that meant long hours of removing debris, scraping, scrubbing, building, and painting. My friends were all retiring, and here I was back to doing manual labor, but this time it was for the Lord. Our faithful church members worked diligently and showed a remarkable level of commitment. Oh, and our six-month lease turned into 19 years, and Buster never once raised the rent.

I was still holding the lunchtime Luv Ya Houston meetings for men. In the summer of 1996, Evander Holyfield, the three-time heavyweight boxing champion of the world, was our special guest speaker. As usual, men from all over the city, some blue-collar, others white-collar, some church-goers, and others who were un-churched were there. Holyfield did a great job. The men, even non-Christian men, could not wait for the meeting to begin. They wanted to see and hear the heavyweight champion, and to make it even more exciting, Evander was in the process of preparing for a big fight. Reporters were trying to get an interview, but instead, they heard the testimony of his Christian upbringing. It was a powerful afternoon, and many people still remember it to this day.

As we drove home after the meeting, Lena and I looked at each other, and she asked, "Do you think we are supposed to continue doing this?" Everything was going extremely well, and attendance was at an all-time high, but I told her, "No, I don't think so. I don't think we are to continue." Lena had been thinking the same thing. Our dilemma was how to break the news to all of the men after fifteen years of meetings. This phase of our life was coming to an end. My heart had been to disciple men, and I had spiritual sons in both the business world and in ministry. But Lena and I, strangely, were burdened with something brand new. A new God-assignment was being placed before us. He was redirecting us to invest in the lives of the next generation, those searching for their identity, those who were often called the "fatherless" generation. We didn't have a clue exactly what it would look like, but we were ready and willing.

Young Radicals, Revival and Stadium Events

A few months later, we launched a ministry called Generation Jesus with some of the young people God had sent to the church. I served as founder, president, and spiritual father, and Lena was the director, trainer, and spiritual mother. Generation Jesus was an equipping ministry and a movement for young people. We held evangelistic outreaches in all kinds of places, from parking lots to stadiums. Young adults between the ages of 16 and 35 attended, and the ministry was done by young people, for young people, to young people. We trained the leaders and raised them up and "pastor-parented" them, I guess you might say.

I had been prophesying that young people would be coming to our church for some time. I knew that for me to say that, being a pastor in my mid-sixties, was difficult for some to grasp. But I believed it so strongly that I began to envision a state-of-the-art mobile soundstage with stage lighting. Although I knew what we needed, I found it challenging to explain to others. I talked with some engineers and even an architect but couldn't get plans drawn up to build it.

One of our church members, the CFO of a large auto dealership, married a man who was a service manager at the dealership. I mentioned my concept to him one day, and he seemed to get it. Then he told me he had prior drafting, mechanical drawing, experience. We met for several evenings while I described my vision, and he did his best to capture it on paper. Finally, we made some progress! I went to generator manufacturers, sheet metal and canvas shops, and auto supply places specializing in building custom sports cars with plans in hand.

I then began to challenge an older generation to help us to take the gospel to the streets. The businessmen of Luv Ya Houston donated thousands of dollars to see each component of our project purchased, then assembled. There were miles of cables and wiring involved. Although I turned 65 that year, I passionately pursued my dream. My friend, Larson LeBlanc, and I worked long hours, even all night on many occasions, to complete the wiring. It was important to me that it was state-of-the-art and built with excellence according to the design I felt the Lord had given me.

A year later, it was finally ready to go.

Closed, it looked a bit like a sleek race car or small plane carrier that we towed behind Generation Jesus's white Suburban. Parked and unhitched, it opened into a full-size praise and worship soundstage with mics, top-notch amplifiers, huge speakers, and professional stage lighting. The onboard generator provided electrical power, and the canvas canopy protected us from the sun's rays and the rain.

We could pull into an empty parking lot, drive down to the beach or any other outdoor location, and conduct services. It was so unique, the state of Texas had to create a special classification to license it. Before long, the young people were holding their first outdoor meetings. They dubbed it "the GJ Trailer." Lena would contact businesses with large parking lots to ask if we could use them for the night. If they agreed, we'd get the necessary permits with the city and proper insurance for the event. We were starting to become somewhat well-known in Sugar Land. Soon our Generation Jesus team took the trailer with its soundstage everywhere to hold outdoor Christian concerts. We would draw 600-800 young people at each of these events. Many of the young people attending weren't going to a church, but through these outreaches, they came to Jesus!

One of these events was in Sugar Creek Baptist Church's parking lot, where world heavyweight boxing champion Evander Holyfield was our guest speaker. An outreach at Crystal Beach during spring break was an extreme success. We set up the trailer there and preached and played music and baptized new converts in the ocean. We had events at Quail Valley Church's parking lot in March of '98 and Jumbo Sports parking lot in April. Those mobile events, and several others, were precursors to what would be our stadium events at Mercer Stadium.

In 1995, when we were still meeting at the Aerodrome ice rink, one of the young men on our team was standing with me as we looked across the way from that facility. We saw the stadium and boldly said, "One day, we will fill it with young people for God." Three years later, we were filling parking lots with young people. So I decided to reach out to the Fort Bend Independent School District to inquire about using the Mercer Football Stadium. I made call after call and spoke to one person after another, but got nothing except a runaround. This went on for months. We learned that the school district had invested a million dollars on new Astroturf for the football field, and their reluctance finally made sense to me.

On January 10, 1999, Lena and I attended a Sunday night service in West Columbia, west of Houston. Dale Gentry was ministering, and he called us out and prophesied to us,

> *"You are going to gather thousands of young people in stadiums. You're going to fill stadiums across this nation with singing and praying and dancing and rejoicing and lifting up the name of Jesus, exalting the Name of the Lord."*

I thought to myself, "Well, I don't know how that's going to happen because I can't even get my calls returned when it comes to stadiums."

The following morning, I went back to West Columbia to hear another speaker. While I was gone, the Fort Bend Independent School District called and, after months of polite refusals, left a message we could use the stadium. We were in shock! The only stipulation was to first meet with the athletic director to let him know what we would be doing. Kyle Byrd, who had a ministry for youth called Frontline Ministries, went with me to see Keith Kilgore, the school's athletic director. When we met Coach Kilgore and told him our plan, he emphatically said, "No! No way!" He was not going to approve it because of the new Astroturf on the field. It had been very expensive, and he didn't want anybody messing it up.

Finally, he said we could use the stadium if we'd agree not to put anything on the field. He was still trying to protect the turf. I told him that we would need to set up cameras and lights on the field, or we couldn't do it. We were at an impasse, so I returned to the church to pray. In prayer, God showed me exactly what to do. I returned to Coach Kilgore's office and showed him how the size and weight of our equipment would do less damage to his turf, in pounds per square inch, than his linebackers would. He agreed and said, "Mr. Jones, you've got it!" To this day, we are the only outside organization ever permitted to use Mercer Stadium for this kind of event. It was a miracle! We had learned how to attract 800-900 young people in parking lots. But how were we going to fill a 10,000-seat football stadium? And, how in the world were we going to pay for it all?

I went and sat in my office, which was the children's classroom, since the kids just needed it on Sundays. We only had 2,000 square feet total for the entire church. The only office was a nine-by-nine space that Lena and everybody else used, so the children's room gave me the most privacy. There were small children's sized tables and chairs, and I sat in one of the chairs, my knees nearly up at my chest, and began to pray. After a few minutes, the Lord dropped the name of a man into my heart who used to attend the Luv Ya Houston meetings. He was a member of a large church in our area, and I had not seen him in years. But I knew he owned some successful franchise stores in our area.

I looked up his number and called it, and his son answered the phone. After telling him who I was, he said, "I'm not really supposed to do this, but I'm going to give you my dad's cell number." That must have been the favor of God because I immediately called the number, and Paul answered on the first ring. I told him how I wanted to do a stadium event for young people in our area and told him my vision. Then I explained about the prophetic word we had received and how we finally got permission to use the stadium but had no idea how to pay for it. He asked me how much I needed. I blindly guessed it would cost around $12,000.00. To my surprise, he said, "My kids and their friends go to those Generation Jesus meetings, and they love them. I'll give you $10,000.00 to help cover expenses." I was stunned at how fast the Lord was providing. I thanked him and sat there for a minute, thanking God. Then while I was walking into the office to tell Lena what God had done, my phone rang. It was Paul, and he said, "On second thought, I'll give the entire $12,000!" I was more than excited, and the wheels began to turn inside my head.

To attract that many people, I realized we would have to offer something for everybody, which was easier said than done. We decided to hold competitions and contests all day Friday, then cap it off with worship and an evangelistic sermon that night. I began to network throughout the county. I met with the mayor, the chief of police, the fire chief, and other dignitaries, including all the county judges.

They all appreciated the initiative we were taking in trying to help the youth. The county judges were so impressed that they, along with other dignitaries, agreed to be the judges for the contests and competitions. We also had many local celebrities participating, with a little something for everybody. People were amazed when they came into the venue to see the low rider cars on display. We had various categories with prizes going to the best-decorated cars. Rudy Tomjanovich, head coach of the Houston Rockets, judged our free-throw basketball competition.

There was a skateboard ramp where pros judged tricks and turns and flips. We had a breakdancing competition that was Lena's favorite thing to watch. Some kind of talent was on display no matter where you looked. The world champion professional yo-yo champ did his famous tricks and gave out free yo-yos. Clutch, the Houston Rocket's mascot, was walking from contest to contest, and people loved getting their picture taken with him. One of our main entertainment attractions was Dennis Rogers, the Grandmaster Strongman, called "pound for pound the strongest man in the world." He is in the Guinness Book of World Records. Dennis demonstrated some remarkable feats of strength. With his bare hands, he held two Harley Davidson motorcycles (hogs) and prevented them from driving away. Billows of smoke, asphalt, and burning rubber engulfed him while the crowd roared.

We drew about 4,500 in attendance. Prizes for all competitions were awarded at the end of the day, meaning no one left. A sought-after Christian band called Human played for a while before our GJ Band led the crowd in a powerful time of worship. You could feel the presence of the Lord when it was time for our ministry team to begin sharing. After a few testimonies, one of our young GJ preachers went to the stage. He preached a riveting message and followed it up with a compelling altar call. Hundreds of young people made public professions of faith in Christ for the very first time that night. And then, with everyone still there, we awarded the prizes.

The event ended up costing $25,000 instead of the $12,000 I had raised from Paul, "our main stadium sponsor." I got the rest in increments from various businessmen I knew, and every penny we needed came in by the time we needed it. All the planning and pre-event labor and work had gone on day and night for three months. It was provided on a free volunteer basis by Lena and me, our one church employee, and our church members and GJ leaders. It was not easy to pull it off, but the young people who dedicated their lives to Jesus at the end of the night made it all worth it.

The following year, we did it again. On April 21, 2000, Easter weekend, we held our second Generation Jesus stadium rally. This time I knew we needed to go bigger and better. And we set a budget of $35,000 we needed to raise, which meant I sent letters to all the former Luv Ya Houston men asking for their help. The kids in Fort Bend county are difficult to impress, and we wanted to attract the unchurched. Someone at the mall overheard one young man asking, "What are they gonna do this year at the stadium thing?"
Another answered, "Maybe they'll have the world's strongest man again."
The first young man replied, "Oh, but I've already seen him." When I heard that, I immediately had an idea. I made an appointment with the Houston Skydive people and asked two parachutists to jump out of planes and land on the 50-yard line of the stadium. They loved the very thought of it! Since we had no budget to cover anything like that, I recruited one of our area businesses to sponsor it. We flew banners from the planes emblazoned with Discount Tires, the name of our incredible sponsor.

The weather bureau had predicted rain for that day. Reporters were asking me, "What are y'all gonna do when it rains?"
"It's not going to rain," I said.
One said, "Oh, it's going to rain alright."

Later, we learned that an eight to ten square block area around the stadium had no rain. Outside of that dry area, they experienced heavy rainfall.

Some people came out of curiosity. They were shocked when they drove into the dry area around the stadium. We ended with 5,000 in attendance, and many young people were saved and gave their lives to the Lord again.

During the evening event, the lights and sound suddenly went out, right in the middle of worship. Everything on stage went dark, so our leaders grabbed bullhorns and kept the crowd engaged. We discovered, to our dismay, the generator had run out of diesel fuel. We somehow had to run and get diesel while the crowd continued to worship. We sent one of our team members with the ministry credit card. However, due to the high number of charges at so many different places that day, the credit card company had flagged our card for possible fraud. Our young GJ team member couldn't use the card to pay for the needed diesel fuel, and, of course, he had no cash on him! After some frantic and crazy arrangements, we got the diesel, filled the tank, and the service continued as planned. One thing was for sure; our life was never boring!

I was 67 years old, pouring diesel into generators at football stadiums while teens and twenty-somethings worshipped. It's good that my early life consisted of so many different kinds of jobs. At least I was ready for whatever came my way in ministry.

Missions Trips, Mountain Lions and Moving

In 2001 we took 16 of our young people on a mission trip to Ireland. They shared Christ and witnessed in bars and clubs, where people tended to hang out for hours on end. Soon they decided they would do "live interviews" with our video camera. As young people came out of the bars at all hours, we were like the paparazzi, ready with our camera and list of questions. Nearly everyone was ready and willing to be filmed. We were Americans, and for all they knew, they could end up on television and have their fifteen minutes of fame. Of course, after a few preliminary questions, we always asked what they believed about God and if they realized they could have a relationship with Him. Then we had an opportunity to respond accordingly. Some kids received Jesus while we were there. We prayed with others and encountered many who were quite curious about God. Since teen suicides were on a steep rise, we felt our visit was at a God-ordained time. And while our camera had no film and was just an empty prop, our hearts were full. We were determined to make a difference in the lives of those we met, many of whom seemed hopeless. Some people couldn't understand why we would take a mission trip to Ireland, assuming it was a heavily churched nation.

On the contrary, it was and is virtually an unchurched society. While it might be considered deeply religious, there is very little knowledge of the power of the gospel of Jesus Christ. One of the young men we took did rap music, and as he began to perform in the town squares, it would always draw a crowd. Our GJ band set up with acoustic instruments on sidewalk corners. As we worshipped, people would gather to stop and listen and stay for a while.

One bystander even threw a few coins into our guitar player's open case on a nearby sidewalk, and we had a good laugh about that. One afternoon, a man who seemed to be foaming at the mouth and quite rowdy tried to intimidate us as we stood and prayed in one of the open areas. He started insanely lunging at various ones and then walked up to Lena as if to knock her camera out of her hands. She didn't flinch, nor did she answer his taunts and just stared straight at him. Then he bumped her quite hard, causing the camera to fall out of her hands and hit the ground. While some of our young guys trained in martial arts were ready to take him down, I gave a signal for them not to move. Despite their apparent concerns for Lena's safety, they did just as I ordered and were completely still. I somehow knew the guy wasn't going to hurt her, and I'm so glad we didn't act hastily or react in the flesh. Before the afternoon was over, Lena was praying with the man, and he was tearfully apologizing for his actions. It turns out he was a former prizefighter in Ireland and had gotten down on his luck and fell into drinking and drugs. His life had spiraled out of control. Instead of our guys getting into an awful brawl with a former prizefighter, God softened his heart. We prayed with him, and we asked the Lord for a new beginning for him.

Later that year, I took a second mission trip, this time with another minister. We went to "the land down under", Australia. He had several speaking engagements, and I was supposed to share and speak at a few meetings myself. Some of the people became convinced I was James Garner. One of the pastors urged us on, so we decided to add to their illusion by buying a cowboy hat for me at a Western store. The store's owner ran out to meet me, thinking I was the real James Garner, and she asked for an autograph to add to her "celebrity corner." I didn't want to sign someone else's name as it just seemed wrong, so I quickly wrote "Maverick" for her, and she was thrilled. That was the television name of James Garner in his Western series that ran from 1957-1962, but spin-offs and reruns kept it alive for decades. I am not sure if anyone ever told her who I was.

I have some great memories from that trip. I remember a coffee shop I loved in Mooloolaba on the Sunshine Coast of Australia, which is absolutely beautiful. The night before we were supposed to leave, we were there in the hotel room, and I was watching television. I thought it was some strange program or violent video game. It was terrorists intentionally flying airliners into a skyscraper. I had no idea, at first, but it wasn't a program at all. Instead, it was REAL! The 9/11 tragedy was unfolding at the World Trade Center in New York, and I was on the other side of the world. You may recall that immediately all the planes were grounded. For a week, there were no planes in the sky except the President's Air Force One. Because of that event and the security measures that followed, we could not return home for at least another week.

In our church's foyer area in Sugar Land, we had a full-color vinyl mesh scrim like the kind you see used as theater backdrops. It was an expansive view of New York's skyline and had been part of an Armani window display at the Houston Galleria, and it was huge. Spanning 14 feet by 12 feet, our young people thought it was cool looking in the entry area. Both of the Twin Towers stood proudly right in the very center of it. Several years after 9/11, people would still stop and look at our skyline, which showed how it looked before the brutal destruction of one of the towers. Until we moved from that space in 2011, people who walked by and saw it would always stand and reflect for a few moments.

I have a good friend, Perry Hardwick, who was and is a major supporter of both Generation Jesus and our church. As an avid hunter, he has traveled all over the world for a hunt. He surprised me in 2003 with an unforgettable adventure for my birthday. At 70 years of age, I had spent the previous ten years planting a church and launching and overseeing various ministries. Much of that work was on an unpaid basis and I'd not had the time or money for things like hunting or fishing, even though I enjoyed them both. He said, "E.Z., I want to treat you to a mountain lion hunt in New Mexico." I was excited and very grateful to my thoughtful and generous friend.

When I arrived in New Mexico, he had arranged for me to meet my guides. They briefed me on how they would do things, and we rode our horses up into the mountains in the snow. We began the hunt with some young "special forces" military guys. However, the temperature dropped to a bitterly cold level. The young guys rode back down after deciding conditions were too severe to go on. Our guides weren't too keen on continuing the hunt.

But at my age, I knew I would never have this opportunity again, and I wasn't going to miss it! So, I bundled up, built a fire, and huddled all alone in the cold darkness. I put tin foil over a fire I made on the ground so it would conduct more heat. It was of the utmost importance that I stay awake all night, or I would freeze to death. But I've never been a quitter, and at age 70, I sure wasn't going to change that. To make a long story short, I shot my lion. To my surprise, my benefactor friend paid a taxidermist to skin it. He then shipped the skin with the head on it to my office. I carefully laid it out on a six-foot-long table desk I had from the late '70s. I now had my own office at the church since we had doubled our lease space to 4,000 square feet. It still wasn't much, but we did more in that small amount of space than some people do with ten times as much. But when Lena walked into my office and saw it, her big brown Italian eyes doubled in size and her shriek…well, we will leave it at that! We eventually found a new home for it with someone who liked to look at it a lot more than Lena did! And I got a great sermon out of my hunt called "Wild

Mustangs and Hound Dogs," and some of my Generation Jesus leaders can quote from it to this day!

The mountain lion hunt would not have been possible for me had I not been in tip-top shape and doing daily work-outs. For years I worked out alone before I started meeting with Joe Landy at the gym near my house and we spurred one another on since we are both quite competitive. He is much younger than I am and became like a son to me. Most people thought he *was* my son. Our early morning gym work-outs were great and I interspersed them with lots of spiritual talks. Today Joe is a very successful market partner for Texas Roadhouse.

Some of my other work-outs were done with Evander Holyfield, who had become the four-time heavyweight boxing champion of the world. He had spoken at two of my Luv Ya Houston meetings in the past and then at two of the Generation Jesus events.

Initially, I got to know Evander Holyfield through Tim Hallmark, one of my spiritual sons. Tim is a world-class trainer who worked with Evander when he first got out of the Olympics and trained as a professional fighter. He brought Evander from his Olympic middleweight class to qualifying in the heavyweight division.

Tim still works with many athletes today to keep them at peak performance. Evander had a boxing gym he used in Houston, so when Tim would train Evander here, he would always give me a call. For several years, I would meet them on and off at the 24-hour Fitness gym on Richmond Avenue and do the work-out right alongside Evander, the same weights pound for pound. And I kept the pictures to prove it. Since I was in really great shape, even well into my seventies, it was not difficult for me to travel overseas on strenuous mission trips.

In 2005, at the age of 72, I traveled to India to help with tsunami relief. A large group of people from various churches and ministries went under one umbrella ministry. One of my spiritual daughters, Cami Mullins, had planned to go on the trip, and she hoped and prayed that someone she knew would go with her. I boldly declared that it wasn't going to be me, but after a unique series of events, God put it on my heart to go. Once we got there, we were introduced to a nation of people who were very receptive to the things of God. India is unlike any country I've ever visited. We unloaded hundreds and hundreds of 50-pound bags of rice and brought supplies of all kinds for the people. Then we held large crusades in the evenings with literally hundreds of thousands attending. We would preach the gospel and pray for the sick. On my trip, there were miraculous healings and many deliverances. It was not at all uncommon on that trip for countless deaf and dumb people to be instantly healed.

After one of the services, people were being ushered to the front for me to pray for them. One was a young man along with his mother. She explained to the interpreters that he was blind. So, I began to pray for him. Suddenly, he began to speak in his native Hindi language. I said, "Somebody, tell me what he's saying." One man explained, "He was blind in one eye. Now he can see better in that eye than he can with his other one." I said, "Take him upstairs and let the doctors check him out." That was the first overseas miracle that I experienced, and in later years there were many more. Little did Cami know that this trip would be the first of several I'd take to India.

The following year, Lena and I went to a three-day circuit pastor meeting Dale Gentry was having in Austin. The meetings were being held in the home of Bill and Sue Hart, who pastored Cathedral of Praise. There were several pastors present who were all connected with Dale, and every session was fantastic. One afternoon Dale pulled two chairs into the center of the living room and said, "These are now the prophetic chairs." Dale's prophetic gift began to flow, and Lena and I loved hearing all the inspiring words the various pastors were receiving. There were words of encouragement, words that pierced their hearts, and words speaking of things God was going to do. It was all so anointed. Unexpectedly, Dale said, "E.Z. and Lena, y'all come and sit in the prophetic chairs if you will." He started praying in tongues and began to speak about how we were called to train eleventh-hour workers. He said there would be young people, and we would commission them to go into all the world. He prophesied,

> *"There are many who will go to Bible colleges and universities. But there are some who are estranged from their fathers and estranged from their mothers, and God will send them to you. You will take them under your wing, and you will tell them they are of value and there is a plan for their life. You will mobilize not just tens or twenties, but thousands of young people, and they will do many signs and wonders. There is a mantle upon the two of you to teach and train these young people. Many will come against you but keep your foreheads like flint because God will do mighty things."*

I didn't let it show, but my heart immediately sank. When we got back to the hotel room, Lena could read right through my normal-looking exterior, and so she asked, "What is wrong with you?" I looked down and said, "Nothing." She asked again, "What is wrong with you?" I said, "That's just not the word I wanted to get." I was 73 years old. I didn't think I'd be doing this same kind of thing all over again. We had done it once, and it had been a joy to us the first time. But I guess I felt like Abraham or Sarah. I was just too old for this. Lena looked sternly at me and said, "I married a man whose intention was always to obey God, and so that's what I'm expecting." Dale had told all the pastors that we were going to share communion the following morning, so Lena said, "You just better get all this fixed on the inside of you by morning."

And by the time we shared communion the next day, I was honestly excited about the second wave of young people that God would bring. I gave myself an "attitude adjustment," and I'm glad I did. Never despise any word that God gives you. Because God will bring His joy with every assignment in every season, no matter how unlikely or unwelcome it might seem to you.

In 2006, I returned to India with Gideon Stanley. Gideon is a local minister in our area and a powerful prayer warrior. He is also a businessman who grew up in India, and he has connections with some of the largest churches there. Allen Clark, our worship pastor, also went on the trip. Allen is like a son to me, and he is the epitome of the word faithful. No wonder God chose him to pastor at our church because though he is very gifted in his own right, Allen is a unique blend of my strengths and Lena's strengths. Allen has our complete trust and is very powerful and prophetic in the way he ministers.

There were six of us traveling since Gideon's mom, dad and sister were also on this trip. Gideon's dad is known as an apostle of prayer in India, and we woke up early every morning and prayed for a while before we left for the many church services and meetings we would do each day. To get from place to place, we crammed in a little car like sardines going from city to city, and Gideon's dad literally prayed without ceasing. But there were times we drove so many miles I thought I would not be able to get out of the car when we got to our destination. I was afraid I might be stuck somehow in whatever position I was in, not being used to such confined spaces.

But at every single place, God did extraordinary things. There were physical miracles and many demons cast out of people.

Some of the churches were small, and others had fifteen to twenty thousand members. There was a hard and fast rule at the larger churches that women were not allowed on the platform or the stage. This rule presented a problem for me because Gideon's sister Faith was my interpreter. I was assured they would provide a male interpreter, but I loved Faith's heart and enthusiasm, and we worked well together. When the first male interpreter came up, I'm not sure why but I just decided to speak in tongues. He wasn't sure what to do, so they sent another man up to the stage after a while. But I just continued to pray in tongues, and after one more gentleman was sent up to help, not knowing what to do, they gave up. Faith was finally allowed to come onto the stage, stand by me and interpret. Immediately, I quit praying in tongues and began my message. I would like to say I changed some things for women in India, but I honestly just wanted to work with Faith because she expressed my message with the same passion and spirit that I wanted to convey.

Another rule I was unaware of was the extent to which the large churches paid reverence and respect to their top leaders. In fact, no one touched the head leader or pastor, and no one ever laid hands on them. They were true "untouchables." But when the Holy Spirit began to give me words of knowledge, unaware of this custom, I laid hands on the leader, delivering the word I had heard from the Lord about him. People looked stunned as if they were holding their breath, and even Gideon was quite wide-eyed. We knew all was well, though, when the top pastor smiled and said the word I gave him was right on and that it ministered to him. And nobody said anything more about my touching him. I guess it was okay since God also touched him.

At a mission conference I attended in Florida a few years earlier, John Artzer, one of my spiritual sons, was looking forward to connecting me with Pastor Andres Bunch from Bogota, Colombia.

He had become close friends with Pastor Bunch when he stayed in Colombia for a while, so much so that Bunch wanted John to stay and help minister at his church.

The conference was great and I was so glad John encouraged me to attend. But at every meeting, instead of getting to know Pastor Bunch, I found myself drawn to Pastor A. Stephen. He had planted churches and ministries all over India and his ministry was basically a headquarters for many of the pastors he had trained. He had also established a university in the city of Bangalore as well as orphanages in various areas.

In 2007 I made another major trip to India, and I worked with Pastor Stephen's ministry, Cornerstone World Challenge. Our church had collected money to drill water wells while I was there. In village after village, women and children would cry and dance in the streets to see running water right in front of them. In 2006 and on this trip, I was there on Thanksgiving Day, since the trip lasted several weeks. I can assure you my meal on Thanksgiving was nothing like what Lena and her Italian family were having. But that particular mission trip was one of the great highlights of my life. I visited several leper colonies to pray for the people there, and I witnessed many astounding miracles. Traveling from village church to church with Pastor Stephen was a joy to me, even though the conditions were not always the easiest.

I actually received a miracle of my own on that trip. A man came up and asked for prayer for his eyesight at one service, and after I prayed for him, I heard the voice of the Lord inside my heart say, "Now what about you?" I immediately took off the prescription glasses I was wearing and never put them back on. I could see just fine without them, but I went to the eye doctor when I got home and told him what had happened. He looked skeptically at me but didn't say much. After the exam was over, he said, "Well, you're right! You don't need these glasses anymore." Every time I'd go in for my checkup after that, he'd call me "miracle man."

Incidentally, John later told Pastor Bunch and his wife, Beatriz, about Lena's series on emotional healing. Lena and John ended up traveling to Bogota in 2007 so that Lena could teach the series at their large church and many pastors and leaders were in attendance. It was the first of many trips Lena would make to Bogota to minister at Pastor Bunch's church and a few others in the area. Later, she established a chapter of Generation Jesus in Bogota for the young people and trained them for evangelistic ministry and outreaches. I accompanied her on two of her trips and, while we were in Bogota, I spoke at Pastor Miguel Castellanos' church. There were wonderful healings during our ministry times, and one little boy who was healed couldn't stop hugging me.

Back at home, I had been prophesying for more than a few years that a healing revival was coming, and it would be marked by signs, wonders, and miracles. We had already seen many miraculous healings in our small church, and people would even come to have our ministry team and staff pray for them. One dad brought his twelve-year-old boy and said they heard we prayed for healing, and they needed a miracle. They were going to the Mayo Clinic the next day because of a tumor on the boy's pituitary gland at the base of his skull. We prayed with him for a few hours one afternoon, and we felt something had transpired in the supernatural realm. They left to go to the Mayo Clinic the following morning, and when he and his dad got there, the doctors ran tests and told him the tumor they had seen before could no longer be found. That was awesome, but I knew there was more. God had shown me remarkable healings and miracles to come, not just for a few but for multitudes.

In 2008, the church was praying fervently from a place of great unity; we felt we were on the brink of revival. During that time, one of our spiritual daughters, Janean, had a spiritual dream she submitted to us. It seemed to signify the enemy would try to hinder or disrupt this move by causing people to "jump out of the boat" or "get out of the vehicle." She explained how vehicles in spiritual dreams often represent ministry. Truthfully, we just couldn't imagine that happening. But one Friday afternoon a few months later, Lena and I were at a Marriott hotel across town for a few days of rest when we received a call from Allen. He said that five people, including one of our worship leaders, had just informed him they were leaving the church. We were in absolute shock! We were close-knit as a congregation, and it was hard to fathom what could be happening. We immediately left the hotel and rushed home. Two days later, on Sunday, we had a guest speaker scheduled. Knowing nothing about what had just happened, he prophesied that our church had just been hit by a Jezebel spirit and went on to preach on that very subject. Jezebel spirits always try to split churches, and I believe this one stopped a move of God that was about to happen. We spent some time recovering from that hit.

Because we were a small, tight-knit group, many people were hurt by those who left at such a pivotal time. The devil is not afraid of people sitting in churches on Sunday mornings or attending Christian meetings. But when people begin to do the works of Jesus and move in power and in the prophetic, you can expect some resistance. Revival is never without resistance, and so that is why we must not back down or give up when obstacles arise. I have always preached to our congregation: Never Give Up, Don't Quit! I would tell them, "Winners never quit, and quitters never win, and excuses are just lies wrapped in reasoning." Maybe all my old football training served me well in my Christian walk because the need for patience and perseverance can't be underestimated. Not if you want to make it to the finish line. Our Christian walk is not a sprint. It's a marathon, and those with endurance and perseverance will be able to finish their course.

In 2009, I was turning 76 and decided I wanted to do something special to commemorate it. I announced to the church that I was going skydiving for my 76th birthday and wanted to know who would like to join me. Several of the young people quickly decided they would go too. My birthday was May 3, but on May 30, six of us were going to celebrate it by jumping out of a plane. There were three guys, Rodney, Jim and John, and two girls, Julia and Veronica. We all drove over to Skydive Spaceland, the same place that provided the skydivers who landed on the 50-yard line at our Mercer Stadium event nine years earlier. All of us suited up and got ready and went up in the plane, and before the day was over, we had each done tandem jumps on our first skydive. They were in their twenties and thirties, and I was in my mid-seventies, but we had a great time. It was quite exhilarating for all of us.

Since I know I will never retire, it's not a bad idea to go ahead and "refire" every once in a while. My skydiving adventure was fun and exciting and added some fuel to my flame! And it helped those young people to be a little braver and a lot bolder. If we are fearful and afraid, we will never obey all the Lord tells us to do. I like to set an example and inspire these younger generations. They need to know that nothing is impossible and nothing is too hard with God on your side, or really, it's more accurate to say, as long as you stay on God's side.

Later in the summer, a few of us went skydiving again. This time, Allen came with us since he had missed going the first time. We brought Pastor Miguel Castellanos, who was visiting from Bogota, Colombia, with us. After he heard my story, he decided to celebrate his birthday with a skydive too. So I did it all over again in mid-July, and that wasn't too bad for a guy who had just turned 76 years old.

The following year I went on a mission trip to Argentina with my spiritual son, John Artzer. A fiery and passionate preacher with a heart of compassion for the nations, John is a vital part of our church preaching team. We were traveling there with Elisandro, the pastor of a Spanish church in Houston where John was often asked to speak. The three of us had gone to Belize to minister a few years earlier and we worked really well together. In Argentina, our contact was Pastor Guillermo who was doing amazing work among the poor. Many of these poor people were immigrants to Argentina from Central American countries and were treated like outcasts while in Argentina. We felt we could make a spiritual deposit there that would benefit both Guillermo and the immigrants.

When we arrived, we got in Pastor Guillermo's very old car. Right away, I noticed there were several interesting and unique things about it. First of all, as we rode to his home from the airport, I could feel water steadily dripping on my right foot that was planted on the passenger floorboard. Several times the car unexpectedly stopped, and it wasn't always easy to get it restarted. When it was time to get out, the pastor would have to run around to the passenger side with a screwdriver to maneuver the door open, so I or any other passengers could get out. If it rained, since the windshield wipers would go down but not come back up, the pastor had to use a string. The string was attached to the wipers, and the pastor would stick his hand out the window and pull up on the string, so that the wipers would come back up. However, this would cause water to get inside the car since the pastor's hand and arm had to be outside the open window to do this. It was all quite interesting, but my heart was moved by the sacrifices this man was making.

When we got to his home, their lovely family was so proud to show us their table and chairs. They had bought a used set so it would be big enough to host us for dinner. Their selfless love and sacrificial generosity again touched my heart, and I made up my mind that somehow, one day, we were going to buy that man a new car! We had several powerful meetings and services together doing team-style ministry. I was amazed at how tirelessly Pastor Guillermo ministered to all those in need, even though there was little or no financial support from these people. At an evening meeting, John ministered powerfully to the men in drug rehab, and prophetic words flowed freely, and men's lives were changed. We stayed in a home in a gated subdivision, and the pastor was always mindful of our safety.

One night later that week, we were at a coffee shop leisurely talking when the TV news showed an overturned car that had been set on fire. I asked, "Where is that happening?" The coffee shop owner replied, "Two blocks from here." While drinking our coffee, we had no idea that the roadway had been blocked by protestors who were rioting. We then realized why Pastor Guillermo had been cautious, because in the midst of what God was doing, unrest and instability were all around us.

It took me a while, but a few years later, in 2014, we were able to provide this pastor with a new car, which had been my desire from the moment I met him. Phil Harrelson, a longtime friend and supporter, responded to our plea for funds to provide him with a vehicle. Perry Hardwick covered all the taxes and insurance. Crazily, we had to have someone "sneak" the $11,000 in CASH into Argentina. We had been warned that Western Union or bank transfers don't always get to the intended recipient. Pastor Guillermo is still driving that car today. I am so grateful for the fact that we were able to sow into the ministry of this selfless servant to help him as he tirelessly works for the sake of the gospel.

No sooner did we get back from our trip to Argentina in 2010 than we got a notice from our landlord of 16 years. We were going to have to move out of our worship sanctuary and office space, our church home since 1995. Buster Freedman, the owner of the center, sent us a message from his office. It basically said, "We love you, but we are being offered top dollar by the dialysis center next door. They want to expand and take over the space you are occupying." We had no idea where we were going to go. Soon after that, Dale Gentry came to speak at our Sunday service. He prophesied that he saw us in a bigger space. Dale went on to say that bigger wasn't always better, but for us, it would give us the ability to carry out the "God assignment" for our lives. He said we would have radical revival services with worship and preaching that would not be like normal church services.

For three months, we looked for a new location and found nothing. There were just closed doors or places that were not suitable for us. We were getting worried and were running out of time. We were given a reprieve when Mr. Freedman graciously said we could temporarily move to a vacant space in the shopping center while we were still searching. It was where a bank had been located, and it wasn't "bigger" as Dale had prophesied. We did not have nice offices, a conference room, or a large children's area like we were used to having. Yet, while in our "bank location," we still had great services and powerful prayer meetings. The gifts of the Spirit were moving, and more of our members were becoming comfortable "doing ministry."

Lena, Allen, and I spent the remainder of 2011 and all of 2012 and 2013 searching everywhere for a new location for the church. With each new place, we would start with high hopes. We'd consider possible layouts for the sanctuary and our offices and the children's area. But then we would hit an obstacle, and our hopes would be dashed. There were a few times, after looking at a space that didn't work out, Allen just hung his head in despair. It seemed like we would never find the place that God had prophesied. Our three months in the bank space somehow turned into three years. Then we received notice from the landlord that another business was very interested in our space, and they would soon be leasing it to them. It was time for us to move out--again! And still, after all this time, we had nowhere to go.

Back in May of 2008, we had attended a service in Baytown where we received a word from a well-known prophetic minister named Ed Traut. He prophesied about how we wanted a new church building but the devil had been against it yet before it was over, he said, our name and our church would be well-known in the city, as if we had free advertising. More than five years later in July of 2013, at another service, he prophesied how we had searched everywhere for a new church location. He said, *"you have looked at so many places, and people don't always know how to take you, but they will remember you and you are a light wherever you go."* Then he added that he saw our church occupying a space for a period of time on the second floor of a building, maybe even having an elevator to get up to the sanctuary. I remember that Lena and I both thought that it was great what he said back in 2008 about our name and church being known in the city and having free advertising. And he was right about us looking everywhere for a location but that part about being on a second floor was the last place that we wanted our church to be! It just didn't sound practical. To be honest, we had hoped it wasn't an accurate word and we decided not to think about it.

While trying to figure out what we were going to do next, it suddenly occurred to Lena that Buck Eaton pastored a church just a few blocks away from our "bank location." It just so happened that they met on the second floor, and there was also an elevator going up to the sanctuary. In the back of our minds, we wondered if this could be the fulfillment of that "unwanted" part of the word we had received. Maybe this was our chance to get it behind us.

MOVERS, SHAKERS, AND BETRAYERS

In January of 2014, we met with Pastor Buck. He was very gracious and agreed to lease us his sanctuary space on Sunday afternoons. This time slot meant we needed to change to a 3:30 p.m. service instead of the time we were used to meeting. It was a bit of an adjustment, but we all got to sleep in on Sunday mornings. We had some amazing services in that "upper room," but we also had some heartbreak.

Our first service there was in February of 2014. Just six weeks later, on April Fool's Day, we were sent an email by a member of our worship team, a young man who had been in our church for twelve years. It stated that our entire life savings, which had been in an investment fund he managed for more than seven years, was all gone! A few people thought it had to be an April Fool's joke. If only that were the case! Investigations by the FBI, the Texas State Securities Board, and the Fort Bend County Sheriff's Department uncovered concrete evidence that the fund was little more than a Ponzi scheme. We were astounded, and our church members were reeling. Some were angry at what he had done to us. Others had known him since childhood and were not sure what to believe. A few had money invested in his fund and were in shock like we were. It had taken us 25 years of economizing to save up our nest egg. The absolute safety of our principal was critical to us. Little did we know, he ran through all the principal we had been investing year by year while we saw phantom gains on the fraudulent and forged statements he sent us. This young man, nearly in his forties, was like a son to us. Lena and his wife talked regularly. His family came over to our home to watch fireworks on holidays. We were at the hospital at the birth of both their kids. It was hard to believe he was now facing four first-degree felony indictments for the deceptive scheme he had carried out for seven years. It was also hard to believe our life savings was now gone. I was 81 years old, and that's not exactly a time to start over, saving for the future.

The financial loss was devastating to us, but the emotional impact and the betrayal hurt us even more. I remembered when I had lost everything once before. I sure never thought I'd be in that same position forty years later; Lena and I felt like the very life was being sucked out of us.

Week by week, law enforcement investigators on the case uncovered more and more details about the crime, and we became more and more disheartened. We prayed for this young man's restoration but we just could not wrap our heads around it all. A few months later, Pastor Buck had a guest minister from Canada come for a weekend conference. She was known for her accurate prophetic gifting. We went to the Friday night meeting, and toward the end of the service, Patricia Bootsma walked over to us. She began to prophesy.

> *"I see that the two of you have suffered a betrayal by someone close to you. You have been grieved by it, but you need to know that it has grieved heaven also. The word of the Lord to you is... DON'T let it change you!! Don't let it change you."*

At that very moment, as she repeated those words, it became clear that this attack was not just on our finances or our hearts but on our specific ministry call. The enemy wanted to get us to enter into faulty agreements and form false mindsets. He wanted us to quit getting close to young people and to quit loving them unconditionally. The devil's plan was to get us to stop investing in the next generation, the ones that God had promised He would send us. That night, we promised God we would not change, but we knew we needed His help to keep that promise.

Our search for a new location slowed down. We became very comfortable renting at Pastor Buck's new location, having our Sunday afternoon services. On April 23 of 2017, in the middle of worship, Allen was singing when he stopped and began to prophesy, "Get ready, get ready, pack your bags, says the Lord. You're about to move!" Then Allen added, "I don't know if that means move spiritually or physically or what… But get ready!" He told me later after church that deep down, he felt it was about a building. But after everyone's hopes being dashed so many times, he just couldn't bring himself to say that it meant that. And he also knew that the Lord's timing doesn't always coincide with ours, which can cause people to have misunderstanding and unbelief when there is a delay or a time of waiting. After all, we had been looking for SEVEN long years.

But, a mere ten days after that word, we contacted a realtor about some space he had listed. When we didn't like it, he took us to see vacant space in another building he had that was for lease. For nine years, it had never been occupied and was in a uniquely visible location. It wasn't in the square footage range we had been looking for, but when we added the square footage to the space that was available one suite over, the total was perfect. It was two and a half times the size of our former location. It "was bigger than we needed," just like Dale Gentry had prophesied in 2010. It also had an elevator and was on the second floor, exactly as Ed Traut had seen when he gave us the prophetic word in 2013.

We then realized it had never been Pastor Buck's second-floor upper room that God was talking about in that word. Instead, it was this location that had been waiting for us: it was going to become our new home. You can't try to fulfill God's word in your own way or your desired timing if you get tired of waiting. It never HAS worked, and it never WILL work! The lit-up sign with the words Epicenter Church all in caps would be placed on the very front of the building at our new space. It was located two stories up on a huge round glass enclosure and was facing a major intersection in our city. Thousands of cars would pass by it daily. Due to the unique placement of our sign, the name of the church "would be well-known in the city" and have "free advertising", which is exactly what was said in 2008, the very same year the building was built.

In July 2017, we signed the lease for our new location. If you had told us it would take that long to get the space that had been prophesied, we would never have believed you.

The unbelievable generosity of an attorney named Debra Hayes made it possible for us to pre-pay a portion of our rent over the entire term of the lease. She had received Jesus at one of our early church Bible studies Lena had for women in the mid-nineties. Debra and her husband Jim attended our church for a few years before attending one closer to their home across town. But we always kept in touch. After a while, she became like a daughter to me. When her law practice began to flourish, she started giving a check to our ministry at the end of the year. For several years, she gave generously to our church. But as we searched for our new location, she was determined to help us even more and gave extra funds for that purpose. But then, very unexpectedly, she became ill. Her transition to heaven came before we found our space, and so she never got to see it. But only because of what she had done were we able to qualify financially for the lease and have the ability to rent the space. Incredibly, after she left this earth, she was still making a difference in people's lives. She was still blessing those who came to our church. And that's what I hope to do--somehow keep making a difference in the kingdom even after I'm gone.

There are some prophetic words, like the one about the stadium, that come to pass overnight. But then others can take years. Sarah was 90, and Abraham was 100 before their son of promise was born. I have had MANY of the things God promised me already come to pass. But even though I'm well into my eighties, I still might have years to go for some things to be fulfilled!

Killing The Giants

After a long and expensive build-out, which was more difficult than we bargained for, we moved into our new church space in April of 2018.

In May of 2018, Dale Gentry conducted our building dedication service. Not only did Dale donate his honorarium that day, but he also raised money from those in attendance to help pay down the build-out expenses. Many who were in the congregation to celebrate with us, members and non-members alike, had given generously toward our new facility. Perry Hardwick and his son, Travis, had donated all the tile and flooring, literally every place the soles of our feet touched! People like Jim Hayes and Joe Ragland, both ministry partners for decades, got acquainted with one another for the first time; it was a day of rejoicing for everybody. I had just turned 85 years old, like Caleb, but what God promised me had come to pass! I was ready to take the mountain. We had a place we could bring people for our healing revival, and we were very excited that we were in our "promised land."

But sometimes, even in your promised land, there are giants to kill. That same month, out of the blue, I started having a few odd physical symptoms. Such things were unusual for me, and the only prescription medicine I ever used was eye drops. I worked out regularly and enjoyed excellent health. I had prayed over my body daily for decades and commanded it to function as the Lord intended. Some blood tests I had done in July showed I was in better health than 98% of people who were decades younger, so I figured I just needed to rest a little more. Then my stomach started bothering me occasionally, and there was a burning sensation I'd have after meals. Lena said maybe it was just indigestion. It was the first time in my life I felt anything like that, so I had her go buy some Tums after we figured out what it was that people took for indigestion. Then I took a couple of them whenever that feeling came, even though I rarely took over-the-counter medicines. Suddenly, my back started acting up, and at the same time, I had a few other aches and pains.

For the first time in my life, I had to start taking ibuprofen a time or two each week. We just chalked it up to being tired from the church build-out and move-in. In mid-August, one of our trusted spiritual daughters had a vision about the enemy trying to take me out prematurely. She saw his big hand reaching out to grip me around my mid-section, squeezing it tightly. She knew that he would try to use disappointment, discouragement, and frustration against me. But she also knew, after she and her husband spent some serious time in prayer, that the enemy would not succeed. When the two of them came over to pray with us, she told us about this encounter she'd had. We covered it in prayer and thanked God that the enemy would not succeed!

We felt that was the end of it, feeling like the vision was more symbolic than literal. Since I was still having various symptoms, we decided a restful vacation was all that we needed. Lena began planning a trip for us to Italy. She decided we would go to a few places we hadn't seen before and return to one place we had loved when we visited previously. We waited until October, so it would be off-season and much less expensive for the plane fares and hotel rates. When we finally arrived in Italy on October 9, the driver made his way to the first little town on our itinerary, a beautiful place called Ravello. I felt exhausted and strangely weak, but we chalked it up to jet lag.

Once we checked into the hotel, my physical well-being became a huge concern to Lena. It was hard for me to stay awake, and at other times it was even hard for me to walk. I was having trouble going to the bathroom by myself, and my physical body seemed to not be under my control. Then I would feel like myself for a little while, and all of a sudden, I would feel very ill again. Neither of us knew it, but the very day we had arrived in Italy, our spiritual daughter, the one who had the vision in August, was cooking at her home. She was at her kitchen stove and suddenly felt a deep pain in her stomach. It was so jarring she dropped the spoon she was stirring with, and at that moment, she gripped her midsection and suddenly had the feeling "E.Z. is in trouble!" She began to intercede for me and didn't stop until I got home.

I now realize that her prayers kept me alive. Things were so strange on the trip that Lena became troubled enough to call Allen. "It's so odd that I can't tell what's going on," she told him. "At times," she continued, "E.Z. looks like someone who is dying, but we know he is healthy and doesn't have any illnesses. His blood work from a few months ago was perfect. I think it's a bad case of jet lag because this makes no sense."

We went on to Sorrento, where I slept in the hotel bed for the better part of three days while Lena walked around the city trying to find medicine for me. I constantly had an upset stomach, and I thought it was just bad indigestion in addition to the other issues. Now I was actively asking for something to take since my stomach bothered me so much. Our last destination in Italy was the island of Capri, a place we had loved when we visited a few years earlier. When we arrived, I laid on a couch most of the time, and when I tried to go to a few restaurants, walking only half a block left me exhausted. Lena could not understand why I was staggering and so unsteady on my feet. Certainly, this was not the trip we had envisioned, so it was practically a relief when it was time to go home.

When we went to the airport for our departure, I had to get pushed in a wheelchair and saw parts of the airport I didn't know existed. They had special rooms where we waited in private areas down unseen hallways. We were escorted onto the plane via an elevator and a unique lift system. These things enabled me to get onto the plane through the special entrance designed for wheelchairs. I couldn't wait to get home and get this crazy case of jet lag behind me.

On October 22, we arrived safely back at Houston Intercontinental Airport. Lena vowed we would never again go on such a long flight since it had affected me so drastically. The second night we were home, I got up to go to the bathroom in the middle of the night. My left leg went out from under me, and I ended up on the floor. Thinking I sprained a muscle since my calf felt like something ripped, I started rubbing on my calf where it hurt. During my football days, I recalled we would rub as hard as we could to get the knot out of the muscle. So that's what I did. When I went to a neuromuscular specialist a few days later, he pointed out that my leg was swollen and seemed unresponsive. Again, I decided hard rubbing would solve it, so I rubbed all the more.

Let me give you some good advice here. There *is* such a thing as being *too* tough. I had been in such good shape and had been well for so long I did not get concerned about symptoms that would have caused other people to go to the doctor. Exercise, work-outs, and muscular therapy are great, but they won't solve everything. Since God had promised me many times that I would live a long life and He would extend my years, I counted on that. But that does not mean the enemy will not try to abort God's plan. The devil is a liar, and we must not be unmindful of His devices. After rubbing my calf for five days, my leg was so swollen I could not even go to church on Sunday.

On October 28, 2018, my brother-in-law Jeff talked to Lena at church and told her she needed to take me to the emergency room. After the service, Lena came home and said we were going to the hospital so at least they could wrap my leg and get the swelling down. When we got there, it looked like we might have to wait a while, but to our surprise, we got into an emergency room cubicle room quickly. Lena and I were both relieved and thought we'd be out in an hour. What we didn't know was that Jeff had called ahead, saying that his 85-year-old brother-in-law was on his way. Jeff teaches paramedics at the college and also knew the hospital director. He told the medical director what he suspected after hearing from Lena what was transpiring with my leg.

Jeff's suspicions were confirmed when the emergency room doctors found a huge blood clot from the thigh to the ankle in my left leg. They called it "complete thrombosis" of the veins in the leg. Immediately, we realized I had not worn the compression stockings we bought for the trip on the eleven-hour flight home. We had gotten distracted by the whole wheelchair escapade, and we were upset with ourselves. They emphasized how lucky I was that the clot hadn't gone to my heart or lungs or brain and killed me instantly, especially with all the rubbing I had been doing. I was grateful we got there when we did because the very next day, I had surgery scheduled to remove a skin growth *on that same leg*. Once they started cutting, it would have put me in extreme danger.

The nurses told us they had "clot-buster" meds that could dissolve the clot, so we were waiting for them to start when a doctor came in with a list of questions. We told him we were sure our long international flight and the lack of compression hose had caused the clot. Then another doctor came in with some other questions about blood in my stools and any family history of cancer. We assured him the answer to both questions was no. He told us that flights did not cause large blood clots like the one I had. He was trying to determine if there might be an underlying cause before administering meds that would thin my blood considerably. Then right before he walked out the door, he asked, "Any black stools?" It was then that Lena looked surprised and said, "Well, you know, it's the craziest thing, but in Italy, he was quite weak, and I had to help him when he went to the bathroom. Surprisingly, I noticed that his stools were pure black. I figured it was probably due to one of his vitamin supplements."

The next thing we knew, I was being admitted to the hospital. We thought the treatment would begin the next day, so we texted everybody at church we'd be staying at the hospital for one night. To our surprise, in the morning, they started a battery of tests to determine the cause of the huge clot. We just wanted them to blast it out but we were at their mercy, and we had to do it their way. They did x-rays and imaging and then two different colonoscopies. There was also a CT scan. Our one-day stay in the hospital quickly turned into five. I had several doctors, a whole team, assigned to my case. On the sixth day, they did an endoscopy to see inside my stomach.

When I woke up from the anesthesia in the recovery room, Lena had a funny look on her face. Then I saw a tear running down her cheek. The first thing out of my mouth was, "I don't know what they've told you, but whatever it is, you can wipe that sad look off your face because I'm going to be okay." She hesitated and smiled sweetly and said, "Honey, they say you have stage three cancer. There is a large tumor in your stomach." She squeezed my hand, and I saw another tear roll down her cheek.

One of the specialists assigned to my case had a nurse who came into the room right then. I asked her if she had ever seen a miracle. She said, "No, I don't think so." I said, "Well, you're getting ready to see one." I just had a knowing deep down inside that God was going to keep His promises to me. He was not a man that He would lie, and I knew He hadn't changed His mind.

It turned out that during our entire trip, I had been bleeding internally from the tumor, and that's why my stools were black. Hospital tests showed I lost so much blood I was extremely anemic. I had also lost 13 pounds in less than a month. At any moment, I could have easily died. Once I returned home, the huge clot could have killed me in an instant. My intense rubbing could have caused the clot to come loose and travel to my vital organs. The "clot buster" medicine would have caused me to bleed out from the tumor in my stomach, killing me as they tried to treat the clot.

The devil had tried to kill me in so many ways, but I knew God wasn't through with me yet. And the vision had revealed the attack, though we never dreamed it would be literal. But the prayer had also revealed that the enemy would not succeed. We had to hold fast to that promise. I had seen many people healed over the years as I laid hands on them or prayed for them. But now, I was the one who needed a miracle.

They did a surgical procedure to put an IV filter in my leg to keep the blood clot from traveling. Because now we had a much more serious problem to address. A full-body PET scan was done next, and the rare signet ring cell cancer, which was known to be very aggressive, was not only in my stomach. It had metastasized to several lymph nodes, some of them pressing on my urinary organs and parts of my spine. The cancer was also evident in other areas. Now all the crazy array of symptoms made sense. The oncologist explained that, at my age, chemo might be too much for me. He thought maybe they should let me live out the time I had left in peace.

This type of cancer has a poor prognosis and gave me less than a 10% chance of survival. Another doctor who looked at my test results asked Lena outright if we were just planning on doing palliative care to keep me comfortable and pain-free at my age, rather than attempt anything more aggressive. When Lena and I told both doctors that I had *many* years left to live, they must have thought we were crazy. Because we kept insisting I was going to live, they scheduled the surgery to insert a port into my chest for chemo infusion. The doctor said the chemo would begin right after Thanksgiving on December 1. The plan was to undergo six rounds of chemo if I could tolerate it. Then afterward, there would be gastric surgery to cut out whatever cancer they could. The chemo would take a minimum of 12 weeks, depending on how sick it made me and how many treatments got delayed. The doctors were clear that the chemotherapy could not eliminate the tumor or the cancerous spread; they hoped it would make it less active. Then during surgery, there would be less chance of it spilling out into my bloodstream. There was a very slight possibility the chemo might shrink the cancer slightly, but that was a long shot. The only way to get this kind of cancer out was to surgically cut it out, which was not an easy undertaking. The oncologist and the surgeon had warned us of what we could expect and what we were facing.

While the doctors made sure we were aware they could only do so much, we made sure to tell them we knew God would do the rest. They weren't sure what to make of Lena and me, but as I kept coming to my appointments, the oncologist was shocked at how well I was handling the chemo. Even though I was one of his oldest patients, I was also one of the few who never got an infection. Making every appointment with no treatment delays, I experienced relatively few side-effects, and those I had were mild. When we told the doctor that we took communion together before every chemo appointment, he looked at us and asked, "What's that?" We then had a chance to share in detail what it was, but this scientifically trained man, whose care for me was both excellent and thoughtful, quickly moved on to his next patient.

Even though we believed that God was in control and the enemy would not succeed in his plan against me, I would sometimes hear Lena lying next to me in bed late at night sniffling. As she wiped the tears from her face, I would say, "It's going to be okay, honey. I'm not going anywhere. God's going to heal me." I just knew I was going to live, and God was going to fulfill every promise He had made to me, even though the chemo was visibly aging me week by week.

We went to church on January 13, 2019, knowing I had about one more month of chemo before they would run more tests before the surgery. We had several visitors that day, and Lena was going to be preaching. Worship was in full swing when in the middle of one song, Allen asked those who needed healing to stand at the front and just let the Lord minister to them. He had never done that before in the middle of a worship set. But I took a few steps forward toward the altar, and while I had my eyes closed as I worshipped, I felt a hand on my shoulder and another one right on my stomach.

At one point, I staggered a bit, and Lena later told me she thought I was about to fall because of weakness from the chemo. Then she suddenly realized I was feeling the power of the Holy Spirit; she was right. All I can say is that I felt intense heat beneath the small hand that was on my stomach. Additionally, I could just somehow feel cancer coming out of my stomach and leaving my body through my head. I said nothing to anyone but, when I opened my eyes, Sandra, our faithful church administrator who was like a little daughter to me, was standing nearby. So was her sister Stefanie, but I wasn't sure who might have laid hands on me.

We finished worship, and Lena preached a great message. Immediately after the service was over, I wanted to tell her what had happened to me, but I saw she was already at the back of the sanctuary, in deep conversation with Sandra. The two of them came over to me and said excitedly, "We have to tell you something." I interrupted them and said, "No, I've got to tell *you* something." I quickly continued, "Somebody laid their hand on my stomach and my shoulder when I went up to the front during worship. I felt intense heat on my stomach, and it felt like cancer came up out of my stomach and out of my body through my head."

I didn't know that was nearly the same thing that Sandra had been sharing with Lena. She told Lena that as she laid her hand on my stomach, she had a strong feeling that a miracle was happening. She sensed the cancer was rising up out of my stomach up to my head, like it was leaving me. Stefanie confirmed that as the two of them just prayed quietly in the spirit during the song, they both had a deep sense that something supernatural was happening. While praying, they looked at one another knowingly because, without any words, they both felt the exact same thing, that the healing was *done*.

Lena said to me, "Oh my gosh! This is what we've all been praying for, but maybe we better not tell anybody yet. It just sounds crazy. Especially the part about it coming out of your head!"

That was mid-January. I was scheduled for another PET scan and endoscopy in mid-February before the gastric surgery. The doctor hoped to surgically remove the tumor and any cancer that spread elsewhere without spilling it into my bloodstream. They also had to remove several lymph nodes that showed serious cancerous uptakes on the first PET scan. On the morning of February 14, while other couples were planning their Valentine's

Day dinner, Lena was driving me to get the PET scan. Returning to that facility brought back memories of the early days of the cancer diagnosis when it still seemed surreal. Yet, here we were, back again, holding fast to the belief that God had taken cancer out of me. To be more specific, "it came up out of my head".

Since it would take a few days before we would receive the PET Scan results, we then proceeded to the surgical center for the endoscopy. I was lightly sedated and wheeled into the surgical room, where they administered the anesthesia. Lena was all alone in the waiting area, eating yogurt. She later told me that a nurse informed her that the procedure was over after about forty-five minutes. But the nurse said the doctor needed to speak to her, which was puzzling to Lena. When the doctor came out into the hallway thirty or forty minutes later, he had an odd look on his face. Lena braced herself, not knowing what was coming next. The doctor said, "Well, this is very unusual… but we cannot find the tumor." A sizeable tumor was on the first PET scan, an ulcerated mass about 2 inches in diameter. Lena's eyes grew large as she asked, "It's gone?" The doctor said, "Well, we just cannot find it, and while we see the site where it was, it's just no longer there. We took some biopsies to see what's going on. Now no matter what, we will still have to do the surgery since any tissue where the tumor was still must be removed for safety."

Lena's thoughts were reeling, and she said to herself, "The three of them were absolutely right. God took the cancer out of him!"

A few days later, the PET scan results came. Miraculously, there were no cancerous uptakes any longer in the lymph nodes or anywhere else. Then we got the biopsy report. Only microscopic traces of cancer were found in the spot "where the tumor had previously been". That is how the doctor stated it on his report.

On the morning of March 15, I was admitted to Methodist Hospital for gastric surgery to remove "the tissue where the tumor had been." Lena and I spent the next eight days there. After having such an unusual Valentine's Day, we also spent Lena's birthday in the hospital. But she was thrilled I was getting this all behind me. The surgeon removed half my stomach to be sure not a microscopic trace of cancer remained on any tissue. But when he got the biopsy report a few days after surgery, he was amazed. He had removed a total of 16 lymph nodes, which filter cancer cells and other harmful substances from the body, and *no* cancer was found on any of them.

I was 86 years old, and since the Sunday I walked into the hospital in October 2019 for "a pulled muscle," I had been under anesthesia countless times for untold hours. In just four and a half months, I had: two colonoscopies, three endoscopies, surgery to install an IVC filter for the blood clot in my leg, surgery to insert a port catheter into my chest, several rounds of chemo, and major gastric surgery. But my mind was sharp, and even though I was in pain and my stomach had a tube in it to drain blood and fluid after the surgery, I knew I would be just fine.

Before we left the hospital, Lena watched the doctor pull the tube straight out of my stomach. Then we finally went home. Recovery is never fun, but after a month or two, all the after-surgery aches and pains subsided. The hole where the tube had been closed up, and I was cating normally, with my stomach stretched back to its regular capacity.

We had experienced many healings in our ministry over the years. But after this miraculous healing from cancer, spontaneous healings started breaking out in our services. Sometimes even as people worshiped, they would feel some heat in their body, and life-long medical issues would instantly be gone. Our awesome children's director, Barbara Chrisman, was listening to our sermon podcast on a Monday and heard a word of knowledge given in the service on Sunday. At that moment, she received it by faith and was instantly healed of a knee condition. We started putting video testimonies on Facebook of some of the people who received healing.

Over the years, Dale Gentry and many other credible ministers had prophesied that signs, wonders, and miracles would mark our ministry and our church. Patricia Bootsma said she saw ambulances driving up and dropping off ill people at our services. She prophesied they would be healed, and we'd have crutches and braces and wheelchairs that they no longer needed, not knowing I had been prophesying the very same thing. It looked like we were on the verge of a healing revival again, even though we had been through quite a storm.

So, of course, the devil tried one last sucker punch to my gut, and I mean that literally. It was about nine or ten months since the surgery, and I was feeling great. But I noticed a slight bulge protruding oddly from my lower stomach. The surgeon said it was some bowel loops, part of my intestines, protruding through a small hernia or tear in the midline incision he made for the gastric surgery. He said it was not uncommon for the abdominal wall, or muscle, to be unable to grow back together well, especially at my age. He warned me it might get bigger, but he said he wouldn't recommend doing anything about it since it was mostly a cosmetic issue. He assured me it wouldn't be physically harmful. Since it would take painful major surgery to repair it, he advised against it. He said that was the last thing he thought I needed after all I had been through. So we wanted to be wise and follow his advice.

Within a few months, it was getting considerably bigger. At the same time, I started having all kinds of issues when going to the bathroom. Let's just be discreet and say it was undignified, very messy, and highly unusual. It kept both Lena and me busy for hours and made her afraid to leave me alone. The thought of one of the "episodes" occurring during her absence was troubling, to put it mildly. She was "on duty" around the clock. Toilet stoppages were a daily occurrence for us, and Lena was becoming physically exhausted trying to keep up with it all. She was still preaching at church, running the household, cooking my meals, and doing many things at our home that I used to do. We would often look at one another and dejectedly say, "This is harder than what we went through with the cancer."

The Covid-19 lockdown began in March 2020 in our area. Even though the bulges protruding from my stomach grew larger each week, we didn't think we should go to the doctor, remembering the advice we had been given. By mid-summer, it began to look like four small basketballs were protruding from my stomach. It started affecting my back and even changed my walk, so Lena made me an appointment with a physical therapist. After two visits, the therapist wisely said she could not permit me to perform the needed exercises. She was alarmed at the effect they had on the "herniated areas" when I exerted myself. She recommended that I see a gastroenterologist right away. Then he, in turn, recommended someone else. Then that doctor advised me to go back to the original surgeon's office.

When the surgeon took one look at me, he immediately said, "We need to fix this." Then Lena started explaining the terrible issues I had been experiencing. She told him, "The bigger the hernia got, the worse the issues became." He assured her there was no connection between the two things. She didn't know what to think when he gave her a medical explanation about how they could not be connected.

On September 3, 2020, I was wheeled into surgery once again. This time it was for a ventral hernia operation. The plan was for me to be discharged either the same day or the following day. But for the next three days in the hospital, I experienced constant, consistent, and nearly unbearable pain at level ten. Since I usually had an extremely high pain tolerance and could handle anything, this was a first for me. Lena stayed with me the whole time, somehow getting past all the stringent Covid-19 "no visitor" restrictions. Securing an elevator passkey, she told me how she was the only "civilian" on the hospital patient floors or in the cafeteria. Everyone else was a doctor, a nurse, or part of the hospital staff. Lena can sure get things done when she sets her mind to it. And she was determined to be there to see I had everything I needed.

My stay ended up being for eight days, and the day before my hospital discharge, the doctor came in to talk to us. He said, "We didn't find just one hernia when we got inside. We found three! And the three hernias somehow caused the colon to get trapped way above them. It was stuck up there, like in a little ball." He went on to say, "We had to release it and give it time to fall or descend back into place before we repaired the hernias." He looked at Lena and said, "When I saw that, I wondered if you might be right about the two issues being connected."

We went home, and within three weeks, the terrible and unnatural bathroom issues ceased. When we went in for our follow-up visit, Lena excitedly told him about our victory. Then she asked, "Are you saying you've never seen this happen before?" This doctor is a well-respected top surgeon who specializes in transplants and high-risk surgeries. He looked at her and said honestly, "No, in all my years practicing medicine, I've never heard of anything like this ever happening."

It was then that we realized it was the devil's last-ditch effort to take me out. In that vision in 2018, our spiritual daughter saw the evil hand of the enemy reach out and "squeeze me around my midsection to take me out prematurely." We just didn't realize that when his first squeeze was not successful in taking me out, he would try a second time.

Knowing that, here's how I see it. I'm ready for twice the miracles now as payback! Since I have been prophesying a healing revival for many years, I guess it's like when I prophesied back in the '90s that youth were coming. It didn't seem likely that youth would come, but it happened. We sure didn't have any idea of all the giants we'd face these past few years, though. Dale Gentry calls it "opposition to our mission." But we made it through.

WHAT'S NEXT

I firmly believe we are on the brink of a mighty outpouring, a great healing revival, in Fort Bend County and the surrounding areas. I believe revival is on the horizon for many regions in our country and in the world.

I have lived a long time, and I have done a lot of things. I've developed real estate, built hundreds of apartments, owned sports teams, traveled on mission trips, conducted healing meetings, planted a church, held stadium events, and been miraculously healed of deadly cancer.

But I am not finished yet!!

I have many spiritual sons and daughters, and I desire that they do much more than I ever have. But I want to leave nothing undone of God's assignments on my life! I will be involved in another healing revival that is yet to come. You are never too young and you are never too old to do what God says you will do! And I am proof of that. It doesn't matter where you come from as long as you let God be in charge of where you're going. And I'm determined I'm going with God full-throttle until I breathe my last breath.

So now the question is--What about YOU? I'm asking you the very same thing God asked me that day in India when I took off my glasses.
What about YOU?
And to that question, I'll add this one.
How determined are YOU?

No matter your age, determine to have faith like a little child all the days of your life.
How disciplined are YOU?
The root word for discipline is disciple, and I want to honor Jesus in all that I do.
And have YOU decided?
Have you decided you won't quit, decided you won't give up, and decided you won't let the devil take you out prematurely?

I'm sure not finished yet.

I have years to go, and I know the best is yet to come.
I'm now 88 years old. I'm sure not finished, and so I'm here to tell you, neither are YOU!

Marine Air Wings   Memphis, Tennessee 1951

In the Marines 1952

Football at Victoria Junior College 1956

E.Z. and John Newcombe #1 Ranked Tennis Player in the World 1970-71

Houston Business Journal Article 1972

E.Z.'s 60th Birthday Party in 1993

EZ and Lena- The Winter Ball 1988

Tim Hallmark, E.Z., Evander Holyfield, and Joe Landy 2001

Mountain Lion Hunt (age 70) 2003

Working Out with Evander Holyfield 2005

Laying Hands on the Sick India 2007

E.Z. and Lena in Italy 2014